Never the Last Road
Samuel Podberesky

"Never the Last Road," by Samuel Podberesky. ISBN 1-58939-416-x (softcover), 1-58939-417-8 (hardcover).

Published 2003 by Virtualbookworm.com Publishing Inc., P.O. Box 9949, College Station, TX , 77842, US. ©2003 Samuel Podberesky. All rights reserved. No part of this publication may be reproduced, stored in a retrieval system, or transmitted in any form or by any means, electronic, mechanical, recording or otherwise, without the prior written permission of Samuel Podberesky.

Manufactured in the United States of America.

IN MEMORIAM

This book is written in memory of my grandparents and the scores of other relatives who I never met because they were slaughtered by the Nazis.

DEDICATION

This book is dedicated to my parents, Noah and Mina Podberesky, and my wife's parents, Samuel and Hela Rubinstein, whose strength, bravery, and will to live during World War II insured the survival of our families. Special thanks must also go to my wife, Rosita, without whose encouragement and understanding this book would have never been written.

NEVER THE LAST ROAD

The title is based on the first line of the Yiddish World War II anthem of the Jewish partisans. This small group of men and women fought to survive and helped other defenseless Jews survive the efforts of the Nazis and other anti-semites to exterminate them. But they also fought for revenge and to leave a legacy that teaches that even the most peaceful and small in number must fight back to overcome the forces of abject evil. Noah and Mina Podberesky were such partisans and this fact-based story chronicles their survival and conflict through World War II and their journey to their adopted home in the United States.

I

It is October 1915 near the town of Vishnevo, Russia, where German and Russian forces are bombarding each other with artillery in their version of the trench warfare practiced during World War I. Huddled in a chamber in a cave, lit only by a few candles, are about 100 local farmers and townspeople seeking shelter from the war above them. The faint rumbling of the artillery can be heard. The only other sound to be heard in the cave is the screaming of a woman. She is laying in a corner propped against a wall with her knees raised. She is surrounded by a man who is comforting her, four young children and two other women who are helping her give birth. After several more primal screams, one of the midwives raises a newborn baby boy into the air, umbilical cord still attached. Inexplicably the baby is not crying and the mother asks nervously about the baby's health. She is assured by the midwife that the baby is well and after the umbilical cord is severed the baby is given to his mother. She turns to the man and children next to her and says "Jacob, my husband, this is our son Noah and children this is your new bother." Jacob kisses his wife and says - "Naomi, you must rest. We will take care of Noah," at which point he takes Noah from her arms. Noah is awake and animated in his father's arms, but he still does not cry.

As time passes the situation in the cave changes for the worse: the sound of the artillery is intense; the chamber trembles from artillery impacts; the candle light has been reduced because of the dust that hangs in the air and the small rock particles dislodged from the roof of the cave by the impacts above ground; and the demeanor of the inhabitants reflects a fear that the cave will collapse or the entrance will be sealed burying them alive. In the corner, Jacob and his family cower as fearful as the rest. As the artillery begins to reach a crescendo, a male figure dressed in a black robe walks carefully across the cave and approaches Jacob and Naomi. He asks them if they know who he is, screaming above the constant roar Jacob says "Yes, I have seen you. You are the priest in Vishnevo." The priest says to Jacob "I know you as well; on occasion I have bought cloth from your store." Jacob replies, "I remember; what do you want of me?" "We are all likely to die soon and I want to save the soul of your baby since he is blameless and innocent", the priest pleads. Jacob answers "Only G-d can save my child." The priest answers, "Yes, but only if you let me baptize your child will he be able to enter heaven." Before Jacob can answer, his wife raises herself on her elbow, stares at the priest and explains to him "My son came into this world as a Jew and when he leaves it he will leave it as a Jew. If after he departs it is G-d's will that he go to heaven, he will go there as a Jew." After a moment of hesitation, she closes her conversation with the priest by saying, "You should pray for yourself and for your flock in this cave; my family and my people know how to pray when they face death. If we both pray, maybe G-d will hear one of us and save us all."

II

It is 1954, late on a hot steamy night in inner-city Baltimore. Many of the Black residents of the 1700 block of Mosher Street are sitting out on their white marble steps in front of their red brick row houses, dressed in tee shirts and shorts to escape some of the stifling heat. The block is only dimly lit by several street lamps except for a brighter light emanating from Nick's Superette Market, a small grocery store with a red, wooden front bordering on an alley near the end of the block.

Inside the store are six people: the store owner, a 40 year old man; his wife, about 35; two young children, an 8-year old boy and a 5-year old girl, all of whom are white and are standing behind a store counter; and two Black customers. One of those customers, an elderly woman, is completing a grocery purchase on credit with the owner, who she calls Nick. The owner's wife speaking with an

Eastern European accent is arguing with the two children telling them they had to go upstairs and go to bed. The boy tells his mother he would rather wait until the store was closed but his mother tells him that could be several hours and it was already long past the boy's and his sister's bedtime. To break the impasse the owner's wife turns and interrupts the owner and asks him "Noah, can you tell Sam to take Naomi and go upstairs to sleep?" Noah replies, "O'k Mina" but he does not have to say anything to the children; his expression directed at Sam is sufficient to get Sam and his sister to leave up the stairs at the back of the store.

The elderly customer and Noah resume their transaction of entering her purchase into a ledger book to be reconciled when the woman receives her monthly social security check. The transaction completed, the woman begins to turn to leave the store but stops and with an inquisitive expression asks the grocer "This is Nick's Market; is your name Nick or Noah?" the grocer responds simply, like his wife with an Eastern European accent "My family calls me Noah but where I came from they called me by a lot of names; Nick is one of the better ones."

Satisfied by the answer, the elderly woman exits the store, leaving Noah and his wife alone momentarily with the other customer, a young Black man who had continued to browse in the store, selecting a few items and placing them on the counter. The door of the store opens again and another young Black man enters while a third man with him stays outside apparently waiting for his friend to complete his purchase. If Noah or his wife would have thought about it, they might have considered it strange that all three men had on buttoned shirts with the tails out in the front. But it was late and they are tired and are only thinking about how hot it is and how soon they can close the store. The man who enters the store quickly walks to the register and asks Noah how much loose cigarettes cost. Noah replies "2 cents each, 3 for a nickel," at which point the man asks for 3 Winstons. Noah then opens a drawer below the counter next to the cash register where the loose cigarettes are kept, pulls out three and turns to face the man. What he faces instead is a long-barreled 38 caliber revolver pointed at his head that the man had pulled from his waist band under his shirt. Ten feet away the man who had entered the store earlier had pulled a similar weapon from his pants and was aiming it at the grocer's wife behind the meat counter.

As Noah stares at the gunman before him he is having trouble understanding what the gunman is screaming and he is also having difficulty focusing on the man's face and the store around him. Noah's past begins to flash before him. In his vision, he is 15 years younger and he still has a gun pointed at his head, but it is not a 38 revolver; rather, it is a lugar. He is no longer in his store but in a forest surrounded by dead and dying horses and men, with others running in all directions. He is still having trouble understanding what the gunman is screaming but he recognizes it is because it is being said in German not in inner-city English. The new gunman is certainly not Black and his shirt tails are not out; in fact, the gunman is a perfectly dressed Wermacht officer. At this point Noah's command of Yiddish and its similarities to German, as well as the added hand signals of the officer bring Noah some understanding; he is to take off and drop the ammunition belt he has on over his Polish cavalry tunic, which has taken the place of his grocer's apron; he is to kick away the belt and his rifle which lay on the ground at his feet; he is to remove and toss away the bugle hanging by a cord from around his neck; he is to raise his arms much higher in the air than they were before; and he is to turn and join the other Polish army prisoners captured by the Germans that day near Czenstochowa in early September 1939, days after the start of World War II.

III

It is a week after Noah was captured and he is sitting in a large compound at the former Polish military base at Radom, where the Germans had taken him after the Czenstochowa battle. The compound is surrounded by a high wire fence topped with barbed wire. Together with him are several hundred other captured Polish soldiers. Along the fence are guard towers manned by German soldiers. Other German troops patrol the outside of the fence.

Several of the Polish soldiers near Noah are discussing what had happened to them in the first few days of the war and are hypothesizing on what the Germans will do with them next. The consensus is that the Germans will either let them go, put them in the German army or use them for forced labor as soon as Poland is defeated. Noah says he is afraid they will face a worse fate. He says that if he can get outside the fence he will try to escape, continuing that he knows his way around the local area from being based there before and from camping there before his military service. Others joked with Noah that since getting outside the fence was not very likely, he better think of alternatives.

The next day Noah notices that the German activities at the compound are changing. There are more troops both inside and outside the fence near his compound, leading to further discussions among the Polish prisoners. Soon, a German officer accompanied by about 15 armed troops enters the compound. He orders the Polish prisoners to line up in formation and tells them they are to be marched to another location. The prisoners comply and when ordered to march out of the compound through a gate to the field outside the fence, they do so. Once the group is about 50 yards outside the fence, the prisoners are formed up once more. In addition to the officer and his platoon there are additional German soldiers on each side of the formation.

The prisoners' expressions turn to puzzlement at the next command from the officer, which is to strip off all their clothes. When a few are slow in following the order, a shot is fired in the air which accomplishes its intended purpose of getting every prisoner undressed quickly. When this is done, the officer directs the prisoners to march away from the compound and their clothes.

After another moment, in rapid succession, Noah hears the officer holler out a command to open fire and the first reports of rifle and submachine gun fire. Most of the prisoners stand frozen or are hit immediately; a number, including Noah, run away from the compound and the ceaseless fire. Bullets strike the ground near Noah, kicking up dirt, and he hears the sound of bullets passing close by his head, but he makes it the hundred meters to a line of trees that provides him some shelter. He does not stop running until he is deeper in the small forest and he must stop to catch his breath. As he stops, he turns and sees two other prisoners who have survived to this point. He tells them that about three kilometers away there is a farm where they may be able to get some clothes and hide for a while. After another moment, with his wind restored, Noah resumes running with the two prisoners following him.

Twenty minutes later they reach the edge of a recently harvested wheat field. On the other side of the field is a modest farmhouse and barn. Noah and his two companions peruse the area as best they can and see no one. They choose the path to the house that will give them the best cover. They try to be as unobtrusive as possible as they leave the tree line and move across the open field. As they come near the farmhouse, a farmer appears from around a building, sees them and from a distance asks who they are. Noah explains they are Polish soldiers escaping from the Germans who have taken their clothes. He asks the farmer for help. The farmer says nothing but motions the men to the barn. After they enter the barn, the farmer comes in and tells them that it is dangerous to be here because of the Germans in the area. He says he will give the men some old clothes and shoes but they must leave at night when it will be easier to travel without being detected. The men thank the farmer and ask him if he could also bring them some food and water. The farmer points to a water trough in the barn and tells the men he will bring food with the clothes. As he leaves he tells the men to stay out of sight and to keep quiet.

About an hour or two later the farmer returns with the promised food and clothes. As the men dress they ask questions about the state of the war and request suggestions on how best to travel to their respective homes. On the state of the war, the farmer has few details except that he knows it is over, Poland has surrendered to the Germans, and the Russians have taken over the eastern part of the country. On safe directions to travel, the farmer knows very little except about the local area but tells the men that from what he has seen, the German army is staying close to main roads, larger cities and train lines. The farmer then leaves promising as he does that he will leave additional food at dusk and pleading for the sake of his family that the men be gone by the following morning.

Noah and the other two men discuss their plans briefly. None are going in the same direction and Noah will have the farthest to go to his home in Vishnevo, which was at Poland's eastern border before the war. It is now hundreds of kilometers behind Russian lines. According to the farmer, those lines are at least a few hundred kilometers east of the Radom area which is located in Central Poland, south of Warsaw.

When darkness has fully fallen, Noah leaves the barn alone, carrying as much food as he can, heading in a generally easterly direction. He walks at night and sleeps during the day, hiding in forests, outbuildings or other safe places. He stays away from cities and roads and tries to cross the busier ones that he must in darkness. He obtains water from streams and small rivers and occasionally stops at out-of-the-way farms to beg food and ask for information and direction. Generally, the farmers hearing that he is a veteran trying to get home are helpful.

After a few days, Noah meets a farmer who has better information for him for his journey. This farmer tells Noah that he is now near the Vistula River, a wide river, that he will have to cross to get home. "Some days walk east of the Vistula is the Bug River which is the new border with Russia," the farmer also tells him.

Noah starts off early the next evening and reaches the banks of the Vistula before dawn. The river is very wide and appears to have a strong current. He decides to rest and swim across the next evening.

Although Noah is a strong swimmer, he learns quickly the following evening that the swim will be long and difficult. Where he enters the water it is very deep and cold and the current makes a shorter direct crossing impossible. After a considerable period of swimming, he realizes he has not crossed even half the river and he is getting tired. He begins to lose hope when he stops swimming and begins treading water to get his bearings. His feet alight on a sandbar just below the water and he is able to stand and rest. Once rested, the remainder of Noah's swim across the Vistula is relatively easy, the water being shallower and with less of a current.

After drying off and resting, Noah resumes his cross country trek. The journey becomes more difficult, not because of the terrain but because as he nears the Russian lines the German soldiers he must avoid become more numerous. Approaching the banks of the Bug several days later, he is particularly careful not to arouse German sentries. Noah swims the relatively narrow Bug River at night uneventfully and upon reaching the eastern bank feels a sense of relief based on being closer to home and away from the Germans.

Noah decides to move away from the river bank. He does so quietly, but the Soviet army sentries are even thicker than their German allies on the other bank and they are patrolling the area heavily. Noah hides, but with daylight, two Russian soldiers spot him and order him out of the bushes he had been using for cover.

They ask him who he is, and Noah, having some command of the Russian language because a Russian dialect was spoken by peasants who lived near his home, responds that he is a Polish worker from Vishnevo who had been trapped in the German zone and was heading home. They ask for his papers which Noah says he lost swimming the river. One of the Soviet soldiers then says, "Tovarish, friend, this is your lucky day; you will not have to walk home; the Soviet army will give you a ride on a train."

The soldiers accompany Noah to their headquarters where he is placed in a small stockade. After a few more days, Noah is marched some distance to a larger prison camp with a number of other Polish men, most in Polish army uniforms. The new prison camp is even more squalid than the one the Germans used. Only the Polish army officers, who are separated, are treated somewhat better, with higher quality food and shelter. In discussions with other prisoners, Noah quickly learns that treatment by the Russians would be harsh, but no one had heard of any mass executions of the kind Noah encountered with the Germans

It is October 1939, six weeks after the beginning of World War II, and Noah celebrates his 24th birthday as a prisoner of the Soviet Union.

IV

After a week in Soviet custody, Noah and the other prisoners with him are herded out of their stockade and forced into trucks. They then are driven for several hours to a railroad siding. Waiting there is a train made up of an engine and several passenger cars in the front and many more box cars in the rear. At the end of the train is a flat bed car topped by a sand bag enclosure manned by Soviet troops. Dozens of Soviet troops also line the tracks and sit atop many of the railroad cars.

The Polish officers are ordered to the front of the train and are loaded into the passenger cars. The Polish enlisted men and those prisoners in civilian clothing are loaded into the box cars. They are packed in with insufficient room for everyone to sit, let alone lie down. In the cars, there is a bucket for bodily functions and no food or water. In Noah's car, the prisoners decide to take shifts standing and sitting. With the cars full, the doors are locked and the train departs, heading east.

A routine begins. The train travels 4 or 5 hours and stops, at which point the prisoners are fed and provided water in buckets. Salt herring and bread become the staples. The routine is regularly interrupted by long waits on sidings as other trains pass. Days of travel turn into weeks. After several weeks, the train arrives at a siding and the prisoners are ordered out. They are faced with their new prison camp. Soldiers order them into the camp where a Soviet officer addresses them. He tells them they are near Gorky which is thousands of kilometers from Poland, so escape is futile. He goes on to explain the camp rules. Except for the cold of the early Russian winter, the unavoidable and ever-present lice, and the meager and bad food, treatment at the prison camp in Gorky is just bad for the enlisted men and only a bit better for the Polish officers. Compounding Noah's misery is the fact that during his weeks stuck in the box car, he had injured his knee and walking without a cane or other support has become very difficult.

Fortunately, after only a few weeks at the Gorky camp, the prisoners are once more placed on a train and moved again, this time to a camp near Moscow. There Noah and the other prisoners are questioned about their backgrounds and homes. Noah tells the truth. He is told that he will be allowed to return to Vishnevo, which is now part of the Soviet Union.

Noah and other prisoners to be released are taken to bath houses to bathe and then are given clean clothes. Again they are placed on a train, but this time Noah is told he will be allowed to leave his box car when it reaches Lida, the nearest mainline station to his home. Polish officers as usual are placed in passenger cars at the front of the train before it leaves Moscow.

After another long ride with a number of stops for food and to let other trains pass, Noah's train reaches Lida, the first stop in what used to be Poland. By this time, Noah is no longer able to walk. Several of the other returning prisoners must carry him off the train and sit him against the wall of the train station. Before the train continues on, Noah notices that somewhere between Moscow and Lida the passenger cars with the Polish officers had been disconnected from the train. Noah asks the other prisoners where the officers were and the consensus is that they would not be as lucky as the enlisted men and would never be coming home.

Noah next sets his mind to thinking of what to do in his current predicament. He begs the stationmaster to send a message to Vishnevo to his older brother Noteh indicating that he is alive in Lida and needs help to get home. The stationmaster agrees. Later that day a message comes back and is delivered to Noah saying Noteh was on his way. Noah then waits, keeping busy by watching the arrivals and departures from the trains transiting Lida.

One train from the east brings a surprise. Alighting from it are three young Jewish women from Vishnevo, Mina Milikowsky, Liba Zalb, and Chirke Milikowsky. Although six years younger than Noah, he recognizes them easily. They also recognize him, but only barely, because of the weight Noah has lost and his overall decrepit appearance. They came over to talk. They tell him that everyone thinks he is dead. Noah tells them a little about his experiences. Finally they ask if they can help but Noah tells them that he expects his brother to come soon to take him home. Mina explains that they are in Lida to buy shoes and will be returning by train later to Vishnevo, and if he was still at the station then, they will help him.

Later that day Noteh Podberesky arrives by train at the Lida station. He proceeds to take Noah to the nearby house of the parents of an old girl friend of Noah's who had married and emigrated to Palestine several years before. Noteh leaves Noah in Lida after the parents agree to let him stay until his leg has recovered. With bed rest, good food and medical care, this does not take too many days. At that time, Noteh returns to Lida to accompany his mostly recovered brother back to Vishnevo. Noah returns to Vishnevo in December 1939, long after his family and friends had given up any hope that he had survived the outbreak of war.

V

Upon his return to Vishnevo, Noah moves into his father's and stepmother's house. His brother tells him of the changes that have taken place under the Soviets. Those affected the most are the large landholders, some of whom have had their land confiscated and been sent off to prison camps in Siberia. Noah asks about Mina Milikowsky's parents, Samuel and Malka, who owned a large farm not far outside Vishnevo. Noteh tells Noah that they are lucky because their workers had told the Soviet authorities that they were fair and honest employers. As a result of these testimonials, the Soviet authorities let the Milikowskys take one of their milk cows and the furniture and clothing they could fit on one horse-drawn wagon and move into town with their children who were still living at home. Noteh continues that Mina's two eldest brothers had been attending Yeshivah in Radun, Poland, near the

Lithuanian border and after the outbreak of war, the Yeshivah had moved into Lithuania where the two now were.

Noteh also tells Noah that in the Soviet system there are no more private businesses in Vishnevo. The government has taken them over. The former owners remain as managers and are paid from the proceeds. That is how Noah's father supports himself. Others find jobs working for larger government businesses. For example, Mina Milikowsky was working as a bookkeeper for a meat processing plant in Ivenets, a town located about 40 kilometers away towards Minsk.

Not long after Noah's leg had fully recovered, he is assigned to work for a government lumbering company near Vishnevo. He is made the assistant bookkeeper and placed in charge of a warehouse used to store horsefeed for the company's operations.

For almost a year and a half through the Spring of 1941, the situation in Vishnevo remains relatively routine and calm. However, life under the Soviets is more difficult economically than under the Polish authorities. Only those with gold or things to barter can get anything other than the bare essentials their salaries provide, but people survive. One bright spot is that there is less anti-semitism than existed when Vishnevo was in Poland and a few Jews are placed in positions of authority.

One day in 1941, Noah sees Mina who is in town visiting her family and stops by to see Noah's stepsister who is one of her best friends. Noah asks her how she and her family are doing. Mina responds that they are all doing well but are worried about her older brothers. The last she had heard they were with the rest of the Yeshivah's students and teachers in Vilnius, Lithuania. They had apparently received visas to travel to Japan. However, while Baruch, Mina's oldest brother, went with the Yeshivah, Abraham Eli, the other brother, had decided to stay behind in Vilnius and try to return to Vishnevo. Mina tells Noah that the family has now lost all contact with them, although they had heard rumors that the Yeshivah had made its way to China and was trying to gain entry for the students and teachers into the U.S. Noah wishes Mina luck and says that he looks forward to seeing her again soon.

As the Spring of 1941 comes to an end, Noah starts to hear rumblings that the 21-month alliance between Germany and the Soviet Union is unraveling. People begin talking about the likelihood of a new war, this time between the Germans and the Soviets. Soviet troop movements near and through Vishnevo only heighten everyone's concern, especially those of the Jews. Noah and others are also hearing stories of Jewish ghettos and concentration camps in Germany and German-controlled Poland. Noah's experience with the strength and brutality of the German army convince him that a renewed war would be a catastrophe for Vishnevo's Jews.

In June 1941, the approaching war becomes Noah's reality. A Soviet officer arrives in Vishnevo and begins the formation of a militia unit of several hundred men from the surrounding area for the Soviet army. Noah, being single, of the right age and having military experience, is inducted. After being given rifles and receiving less than a week of training, the unit begins a march east past Gomel and towards Smolensk where the officer says they will join a larger unit and receive more training. Noah notices increased military activity in the air and on the ground as his unit marches east. Soon the unit learns from people it passes on the road that the war has begun.

Several days later, Noah sees that his unit is approaching a military checkpoint set up on the road. As the militia unit gets closer, Noah first sees that the checkpoint is supported on both sides of the road by dug in and heavily armed troops and two very small tanks. Soon his unit is close enough to see the men at the checkpoint clearly only to discover that they are German paratroops and that the militia unit is outmanned as well as outgunned. When the unit turns to retreat they find that some German troops had also gotten behind them. Without a shot fired this battle ends with surrender.

The Germans having more important concerns than this rag tag unit, order the Soviet soldiers to drop their weapons and ammunition and to turn and march southeast to Minsk where they would be placed in a POW camp. The unit complies.

As the unit marches towards Minsk through farmland, Noah sees that the Germans now control the countryside in force. Noah is unfamiliar with the area, which is made up of flat farmland offering no opportunity to hide or escape. Once the unit reaches the outskirts of Minsk several days later, Noah slips away from the rest of the unit and looks for a way to return to Vishnevo. At first he is lucky, finding a recently abandoned house with food still on the kitchen table, which he devours. Soon he learns why the house and the area around it are abandoned. German troops are sweeping the area for Soviet soldiers and communist officials. Noah tries to sneak out of the area but before long he is spotted by two German sentries. They order him to stop and then take him to an enormous POW camp populated by tens, if not hundreds, of thousands of Soviet prisoners.

It is late July 1941 and Noah is a prisoner of the Germans for the second time in less than two years. Although Minsk is only about 100 kilometers from Vishnevo, Noah has lost hope of surviving, let alone returning home.

VI

The prison camp at Minsk is surreal. It is located in a large open field and is surrounded by German troops. It is filled with a sea of humanity, mostly Soviet soldiers but also many civilians who apparently were communist leaders. Food is skimpy and hard to find and the camp is totally disorganized. Fortunately, late July and August in Minsk is not hot or frigid, so staying out in the open is not too uncomfortable except on the coldest nights.

Noah spends his time walking around the camp looking for food or a means to escape. After a few days he bumps into an old friend from Vishnevo, Abrasha Gorden. They set up a routine where they take turns searching for food around the camp for the two of them.

One day Abrasha comes back from a foray and tells Noah that he has seen Noah's cousin, Dr. Lipa Berkman, tending to sick and wounded prisoners. Noah tells Abrasha that he remembers Lipa and his family living in Vishnevo before they returned to their home in the Soviet Union in the 1920's.

Noah tells Abrasha that he is going off to join his cousin who hopefully is being treated a little better because he is a doctor. When Noah finds his cousin, Lipa puts him to work as a nurse. The next day the Germans order all the doctors and nurses out of the camp. The Germans then separate the doctors and nurses. Noah begins to go with his cousin who stops him and tells him to join the nurses. Lipa says, "all the doctors and Jews will be killed; stay with the nurses and you may live."

After joining the nurses, they are marched to a hospital that had been severely damaged during the German bombardment of the city. Part of the hospital is still operating but the damaged part is full of dead and dying people. The prisoners are told to clear out the rubble and remove the dead bodies and bury them.

Noah works about a week doing this until one day he is told to go to the working part of the hospital to remove a dead body there. Noah knows that the people being treated in this part of the hospital are Germans or Polish or Belarus collaborators. Upon entering the ward where the dead man is lying, Noah is told to remove the man's civilian clothing along with the body. He carries the body out of the ward and when he finds a private spot, he searches the man's clothing. To his surprise he finds German travel papers in one of the pockets. The dead man's papers say he is from Bialystok in what had been Poland, and the Germans had allowed him to travel to Minsk on government business. Noah shoves the dead man's papers in his pocket and disposes of the body, but he keeps the man's clothes.

Later, Noah sees a chance for a successful escape. He first changes into the dead man's clothes. Next he removes the man's picture from his travel papers and replaces it with a picture of himself that he took with him when he left Vishnevo in June. After spending some time memorizing his new name and other details on the travel papers, he is quick to leave the hospital area and begin his return to Vishnevo yet once again.

Several times German troops stop Noah in Minsk but his new papers and his explanation that he is returning home make his escape from the city successful. Noah next plans the rest of his escape. Normally, Noah would have proceeded off the roads to stay away from the Germans, but the land between Minsk and Vishnevo off the main road and away from the small towns that line it is very uninviting. Stretching west and north between Minsk and Vishnevo is the mostly uninhabited Naliboki forest and swamp covering thousands of square kilometers. Noah considers it too dangerous and unwise to cross the Naliboki without a gun and food, especially since his new papers seem to work so well. He uses the road to return to Vishnevo.

As Noah expects, his papers are accepted as he travels the 100 kilometers on the road that leads from Minsk through Rakov and Voloshin and on to Vishnevo. When asked by the German troops he passes what he is doing there, he says in Polish he is returning to Bialystok and he is walking to the main train line that goes to that city. However, when he reaches Pershai, very close to Vishnevo, he believes his ruse has been discovered.

As he walks down a dusty stretch of road, a German field car comes toward him from a distance. It pulls up 20 paces in front of him and two SS non-commissioned officers get out with their weapons pointed at him. They ask for his papers which he produces. They ask him for his name and where he is from. He answers in Polish. They then speak to each other in German. Noah understands enough to realize that the senior SS soldier is saying to let him go while the other is saying that Noah is a Jew and they should shoot him. Noah merely stands, says nothing and gives no indication that he understands what is being discussed. After a moment more of discussion about whether Noah looks Jewish, the senior SS man tells Noah to move on. Noah walks away at a leisurely pace as the SS men watch. Noah keeps on walking at a steady pace, seemingly unperturbed, as one of the men calls out in German, "Stinking Jew, turn around." Noah avoids the reflex to turn and keeps on walking as he hears the car drive off.

That night Noah reaches Vishnevo and goes directly to Noteh's house. It is September 1941 and it is the second time Noah Podberesky, long thought to be dead, has returned to the small town.

VII

The next day Noteh tells Noah about the changes that have taken place in Vishnevo, none of which are good for the Jewish community. The Germans are treating the Jews like animals -- often beating them without provocation. Gold, jewelry and other property is taken from them under threat of death. Jews must all wear a Star of David whenever they are outside their houses. They are not allowed to walk on the sidewalks in the town; instead, they must walk on the muddy or dusty streets. The only exception to this latter rule is Noah's 98 year old grandfather Itcha Ber Berkman, who notwithstanding German threats and family advice, continues to use the sidewalks. The Germans and local townspeople tolerate his act of resistance as an eccentricity.

The government has also changed for the worse, Noteh explains. The Germans have appointed the most virulent anti-semites in the town to official positions, including the mayor and chief of police. Jews and gentiles are no longer allowed to do business with each other. Noah asks how it is possible for the many Jews who depend on trade with the Gentiles to survive. Noteh responds that they are now dependent on their savings, black market barter with the Gentiles, or charity from the remainder of the Jewish community.

In addition, Noteh explains how the Jewish community is run. When the Germans took control of Vishnevo, the community was told that it would take care of itself and be run by a committee that it elected -- a Judenrat. Gedalia, Noah's other brother, is one of its members. All German interactions with the community are through the Judenrat. Among the Judenrat's duties are to make sure no one in the community goes without food or available medical care and to do this it levies taxes on the community. Noteh continues that the Judenrat is also responsible for gathering slave labor work details for the Germans. Regularly, the Germans order large groups of men and women to leave the town to work on various jobs. Men are routinely assigned to the Bogdanova train station and the Vigan railroad freight yards, 5 and 10 kilometers away from Vishnevo, respectively, to load and unload trains. Men are also assigned to the Bukatova area, about 15 kilometers from town, to cut down trees on the edge of the Naliboki forest to be transported to Germany for use as lumber. Other slave labor details are sometimes assigned to repair roads or railroad tracks in the area. Often the work details stay away from Vishnevo for extended periods, sleeping at the work sites under guard to conserve energy and time.

Women are also sent to these places to prepare and serve food and provide water to the workers. Two women, Mina Milikowsky and Shana Zelda Abramovitch, Noah and Noteh's stepsister, work for the area's German army detachment stationed near Bogdonova. There they cook, wash and clean for the Germans.

Finally, Noah asks Noteh what he thinks will become of the Jews in Vishnevo. Noteh is very pessimistic based on what he hears, including Noah's story of the massacre of the Polish army prisoners, but he sees no alternative to continuing to cooperate. He asks Noah what he thinks. Noah is virtually certain that the Jews in Vishnevo will eventually be killed or be sent away to a concentration camp, but he also is at a loss on what they can do. They are 3000 kilometers behind enemy lines and, for the most part, the local population hates them as much as the Nazis. Noah asks about escaping to the Naliboki and hiding. Noteh replies that almost all the Jews in town are either elderly or children who could not survive in the forests or are adults, like Noteh and his wife, who are responsible for taking care of their own parents and children. Noteh knows that a few Jews are already hiding in the forests and he believes a few of the remaining single young adults are considering escape to the Naliboki but he is concerned that, if they do, the

Germans will retaliate against the rest of the community.

Noteh also passes on to Noah that the Naliboki is now much more dangerous than it ever had been before. Polish AKA partisan units, who are more interested in killing Jews and communists than Germans, roam the fringes of the Naliboki. He has also been told by local farmers who sell food to the Jews that the Naliboki is full of ex-Soviet soldiers, mostly Russians and Ukranians, who escaped there after the initial German advance into Russia three months earlier. At present Noteh says these soldiers who, congregate in small groups, remain well armed but are totally disorganized. They are most interested in stealing food, guns and ammunition and avoiding the Germans and the AKA. Any Jews leaving for the Naliboki, in Noteh's view, will quickly fall prey to these violent groups. Noteh's final advice to his younger brother just reinforces what Noah already knows: "when you see that the day has come to stay in Vishnevo and die with your family or to escape, choose to live. Up to now, you have been good at surviving. Survive once more to tell our story."

With his brother's advice, Noah begins to live by Nazi rules in Vishnevo. He spends much of his time loading lumber at the Vigan rail yard, while living with his brother and his family. Noah often sees the Nazis and the local police punching and kicking Jews, but in October he sees the first real indication in Vishnevo that his experience at Radom with Nazi brutality was not an aberration.

Early one morning in October after Noah finishes his breakfast in his brother's house he hears a commotion outside. Looking out carefully from the curtains of a window he sees a group of SS troops moving from house to house calling out certain Jews and taking them into custody. Other Jews are selected in the street. Accompanying the Germans is the town's Gentile tailor, a known anti-semite who seems to be telling the Germans who to select. After rounding up about 25 men, including Mina Milikowsky's uncle, and a woman, who is the tailor's former landlady, the Germans march them towards the Jewish cemetery outside of town. Several hours later, the group is marched back.

Later that day Noah asks his brother what this episode means. Noteh tells Noah that the group of Jews, in fact, had been taken to the cemetery and each had been forced to dig a grave. Noteh has no explanation for the incident but he hopes that it is just a gruesome method of intimidation.

The next morning, the incident repeats itself. The Germans again round up the same group of people and march them toward the cemetery. However, this time about a half hour later Noah hears a series of shots and the group of people do not return. Later, Noah hears from his brother, Gedalia, that the Judenrat was required to send several other Jewish men to fill in the graves of the dead, all of whom had been shot in the head over the grave they had dug. The Germans never explain the senseless killings to the Judenrat.

In early November 1941, shortly after the killings and the Jewish High Holidays, German troops and local police create the Vishnevo ghetto. They force the Jews not living on a two-block stretch of Vilna Road, about a third of the community of 1,000, at gunpoint and with strokes from batons to leave their homes and move into houses on that road. Most move in with relatives. The Judenrat assigns shared housing to those with no families. The move is completed during the daylight hours of one day. The displaced families must leave most of their possessions behind. During the days after the move, a fence is built around the ghetto and a new order is issued that any Jew caught outside the ghetto who is not in the custody of a German soldier will be immediately shot. The Jews watch from behind the fence as first the troops loot the abandoned houses before they are taken over by the local Gentile population.

Noah continues to do what he is told while controlling a mounting anger over the horrible treatment he, his family and friends must endure. He spends as much time as he can in the ghetto with Mina, building a relationship that would have been unlikely before the war because she was from a wealthier family and he was not financially successful. Because Mina works around the Germans near the Bogdanova station, she sometimes hears them talking about the state of the war and she passes on to Noah what little she hears. Most of the news is bad. The war in Russia in late 1941 and early 1942 seems to be going very well for the Germans, and the Japanese have joined the Germans as allies. Local farmers Mina encounters whisper stories of massive Jewish massacres and deportations from larger cities. On the other hand, Mina sometimes overhears the Germans talking about their troops being attacked by "bandits" and she senses that the Germans are afraid to enter or patrol near the Naliboki. Also, a general directive is received in the camp ordering German troops to stop using Jews to do their cooking, which Mina construes as evidence that somewhere a brave Jewish woman poisoned the German soldiers for whom she toiled. All-in-all, Mina says she is not treated very badly; she does not have to do heavy backbreaking work like Noah and she eats relatively well, having access to the German leftovers. In fact, the German soldiers she works for may have even saved her life by ordering that she leave Vishnevo and arrive at work several hours early on the day of the graveyard massacre, making certain that she would not be one of those killed.

Noah and Mina share their hopes and dreams when they talk in the ghetto. He, as he has for many years, maintains his dream to emigrate to Palestine and work on a kibbutz. She looks forward to the war's end so that she and her family can return to their farm near Bukatova and resume their normal lives. Both agree that these are good dreams, but unfortunately reality has placed them in a nightmare.

VIII

It would be incomprehensible in a sane world, but by August 1942, after nine months in the Vishnevo ghetto, Noah's life has become routine: doing the slave labor commanded by the Germans, eating, sleeping, and resting when he can. This morning, two weeks before the High Holidays, the day begins like a number of others with German troops and local police entering the ghetto and rousting out all the residents for a roll call in the square in front of the synagogue. But a number of things are different: there are many more German soldiers and many are SS troops that are new to the town; the troops and police are being considerably more forceful in gathering all the Jews, forcing everyone including invalids out of their houses; and the mayor of the town, Turunsky, a former school teacher, is plainly visible standing in a German army field car conversing in a jocular fashion with two SS officers who are overseeing the activities. These differences concern Noah and he becomes especially alert.

When Noah and the rest of the Vishnevo Jews reach the square, his brother and the rest of the Judenrat are seated at a table as usual to conduct a roll call. Also in the square are a dozen Jewish men from Kreve, a nearby town, who make up a road work detail that had spent the night in the Vishnevo ghetto so their guards could rest. The roll call begins and some people sensing the new danger that Noah also feels become visibly frightened. Others begin to cry. When the roll call reaches the name of the town's Rabbi, there is no answer. The head of the Judenrat tells the German SS officer standing to the side of the table that the Rabbi is probably still praying in the synagogue. The officer turns to an SS soldier nearby and mumbles a few words to him as he leaves to enter the synagogue. Seconds later the synagogue door closes behind the soldier, a shot rings out, and the soldier exits.

The killing of the Rabbi is the final message to most of the Jews in the square that they are about to die, or as some wishfully prayed, to be deported. One woman becomes hysterical and begins screaming about their impending death, at which point the SS officer in charge quietly walks up to her, pulls his lugar from the holster on his hip, without uttering a word shoots her once in the forehead, and calmly turns and orders the roll call to proceed.

Virtually every Jew in the square is now either crying or praying. Noah hears the audible sound of hundreds of men, women and children repeatedly whispering the age old prayer of those Jews facing death: "Shemai Yisrael; Adono Elohainu; Adono Echad. Hear O'Israel; the Lord is our G-d; the Lord is one." Noah also says a prayer but he continues to look for a means of escape. As the roll call continues to its conclusion, Noah notices that a few young adults, including Mina and his stepsister, are counted as still being on work details outside town. That they might survive brings him some comfort.

With the roll call over, the SS officer orders the Jews to line up and march out of the ghetto single file. But before the soldiers can begin moving the people, a German army sergeant standing to the side requests permission to speak, to which the SS officer agrees. Noah understands much of what the sergeant is saying. He begs the officer to allow him to leave Vishnevo in his truck with the Kreve Jews over which he has custody. "They are good workers who are doing important work for the war effort," he says. The officer reluctantly agrees after some arguing, and the Kreve men are quickly loaded into their truck waiting outside the gates of the ghetto next to the square.

The Vishnevo Jews are then forced to march out of the square single file. Most of the adults are carrying young children or invalids or are helping older children and the elderly. The first building they pass outside the ghetto is the home of the town druggist, who Noah sees is inexplicably sitting in front of his house with his family watching the Jews leaving while playing a happy song on a little accordion. As the Jews walk down Kreve Road, Noah sees that most of the other gentile townspeople are either lining the streets looking on or are staring out of their windows. Some are joking and seem happy; others stare on impassively. Noah continues to hear Hebrew prayers being said by those Jews in line near him who are all members of his immediate family. His own prayers also continue. After several blocks they reach the point where Kreve Road leaves Vishnevo. The last building they pass is an unfinished wooden house. Parked next to the road thirty meters past the house is a German army truck that is backed onto the edge of a large corn field which has been harvested for at least one hundred meters into the field. In back of the truck is a table on top of which is a large caliber machine gun. SS troops man the machine gun and the sides of the field along with the local police. Noah only sees a few other trucks, putting to rest any residual hope he has that the Germans are going to relocate the Jews to another location.

The Jews are lined up in rows of 30 or 40 people, one row behind the other. Noah hears the wailing and sobbing reaching a crescendo as he takes his place in one of the back rows. Some people comfort their children; others close their eyes, say their final prayers and resign themselves to their coming death. Noah's eyes, however, continue to dart around looking for any chance to escape. The Jews awaiting their fate are not left waiting long.

The SS officer in charge shouts out one sharp order and the machine gun opens fire. Noah hears the shout and turns and runs as the bullets start flying. People are falling and screaming as he passes them. Bullets whiz by his head and kick up dirt near his feet as he runs at full speed toward the uncut corn. As trained in the army, he runs a zig-zag course, falling to the ground whenever the shells get too close. When he falls, the gunner turns his attention to those still standing or running. Noah then jumps up and sprints again, repeating the tactic. Against all odds, Noah makes it to the uncut corn and runs in twenty or thirty meters and hides as best he can.

After a few more moments the shooting stops and Noah can hear several soldiers coming to the corn field. They check for escapees using the bayonets on their rifles to probe the undergrowth narrowly missing Noah. After a few minutes, they leave the uncut corn to return to the scene of the massacre shouting to their accomplices that no one escaped.

Noah moves up and sees SS soldiers moving among the bodies lying on the ground and shooting any that move or otherwise seem alive. The local police and troops then carry the dead bodies to the nearby unfinished building. The building is set afire and the remaining bodies are dumped into the flames. Then Noah hears the screaming of children and sees Nazi troops carrying Jewish toddlers and young children to the house and throwing them alive into what is now an inferno.

Noah lies in the cornfield for several more hours as the flames devour the Jews of Vishnevo. He watches as the truck with the Kreve Jews drives off. Later he watches as the SS killing unit reforms and drives off in its trucks and field cars to the next town it had to make Judenrein.

As night falls, Noah moves off carefully, escape being his instinctive response, but with the agonized faces of his murdered father, brothers, sister, cousins, nephews, and nieces drowning him in grief and despair. Noah's time of waiting, hoping and praying is over; if he lives, he will do what he can to avenge the slaughter. The burning Jewish children of Vishnevo cry out to him for revenge.

IX

Slowly and quietly, Noah makes his way from the Vishnevo killing field. Before leaving, he tears off the Star of David he had worn for 10 months. Under cover of darkness, he wends his way past the nearby farmers' houses and through Vishnevo's Christian cemetery. He crosses the Alshanka River several kilometers from Vishnevo and quickly reaches the protection of the forest there.

Noah is heading in the direction of the Bogdonova station and he follows a railroad spur line, staying just inside the tree line to maintain his cover. After several hours he reaches the forest near Bogdonova hoping to find escapees from Jewish work details. He hides there for days taking beets, potatoes and corn from the fields, stealing other food from local farmers, and consuming whatever he can find that is edible in the forest.

Eventually, he decides he must approach someone for help. Noah knows a well-off Christian farmer in the area, Solyzynsky, who had cordial relationships with the local Jews for many years before the war. Noah approaches Solyzynsky's farm early one evening and gets his attention when he is returning from working in his fields. Solyzynsky recognizes Noah as one of the town's Jews and asks what he wants. Noah asks if he has seen any other Jews alive in the past few days and, if so, where they can be found.

Noah's spirits are noticeably lifted when Solyzynsky tells Noah that several other Vishnevo Jews are alive. In response to Noah's question about their names, Solyzynsky says he only knows the name of one. He continues that several of the Jews escaped from the Vigan labor camp and two women, including Samuel Milikowsky's daughter, had escaped from the SS barracks at Bogdonova. Noah questions whether Solyzynsky is sure one of the people is Mina Milikowsky and he asks what the other woman looks like. Solyzynsky describes the other woman who is clearly Noah's stepsister. As for the Milikowsky woman, Solyzynsky says he only remembers her from visiting the Milikowsky farm and does not know her name. But from his description of her, Noah knows it is Mina.

As requested, Solyzynsky provides directions to a small hut about a kilometer into the forest. Solyzynsky warns Noah that the area is dangerous, that the Germans and local police are searching for escaped Jews, and that the AKA regularly looks for Jews and Soviet soldiers to kill in the woods near the towns. Deeper in the Naliboki, according to Solyzynsky, are many well-armed ex-Soviet soldiers who are beginning to become more organized and are on occasion raiding local farms for food. Solyzynsky's recommendation to Noah is to be careful and stay hidden in the forest.

Noah thanks Solyzynsky and heads into the forest in the direction that had been pointed out. After a short hike and some searching in the thick woods, he sees the hut. As he gets closer he can see a group of people sitting near it in the brush. Noah calls out in Yiddish who he is and a voice responds in Yiddish to come forward. Seven young adults come forward to meet Noah -- Mina, Shana Zelda, Berke Stoller, Noah's cousin, Bare Michel Rubin, Mina's cousin, Chiena Rabinovich, and Gedalia Dudman.

For the next several hours the small group questions Noah about the slaughter of the Vishnevo Jewish community. Up until then they had heard about the slaughter only in vague and general terms from farmers whose stories had been enough to convince them to slip away from their slave labor details. Now Noah is expected to fill in the details. Everyone there has lost parents and siblings and Noah's details about what happened is too much for several to bear without breaking down and sobbing.

After Noah completes his description of the slaughter, he asks the group how they got together and are surviving. They explain that the five escapees from Vigan and Mina and Shana Zelda were bought together by Solyzynsky. As for surviving, that is difficult, they say. Like Noah, they scavenge for and steal food and keep hidden during daylight hours. They never, however, feel safe because the AKA and the Germans are looking for them and, from Solyzynsky, they know that the German's have been questioning local farmers about Jews hiding in the forest.

No further words are said as it is understood by all that Noah will become a part of this group, the last seven surviving Vishnevo Jews. Noah then turns to his step-sister and provides her some final details about their lost family. Before resting Noah sits down with Mina alone to console each other. Mina is especially distraught because she blames herself for her younger brother Eliachim's death in Vishnevo. Mina explains that while assigned from the Vigan labor detail to work at Bogdonova several days before, Eliachim had told Mina that if the Germans let him return to Vishnevo he would go so he could see their parents. Mina says she already had a premonition that the Germans were soon going to liquidate the ghetto. However, Mina did not have the strength to tell her brother not to go, thinking instead that his visit would comfort his parents. Mina tells Noah that her feelings of guilt overpower her and that she dreams of her brother's decision and her inaction every night. Noah's answer is straightforward: that the decision to return was Eliachim's, that Mina was not likely to have been capable of changing his mind, that there was no guarantee that he would have been able to escape from Vigan, and that, even if he had, his chances of surviving and avoiding further suffering would have been no better than theirs. Mina acknowledges the truth of what Noah says but is not consoled.

Noah changes the subject to something he hopes is more positive and asks Mina how she and Shana Zelda escaped. Mina tells him that, 4 or 5 hours after the SS unit left Bogdonova in the morning , several local farmers walked past the building in front of which Mina was working. They confided in Mina that the Jews in Vishnevo had all been killed. After the shock passed, Mina told the horrible story to Shana Zelda and they decided to run off. According to Mina, she and Shana Zelda also headed towards the Solyzynsky farm several kilometers away, but before they got there, they met Solyzynsky's sister. They begged her for help and she directed them to a nearby barn where she told them to hide. Mina continues that when they entered the barn, they climbed into the loft and burrowed into a pile of hay, thinking they would stay until the night and then run to the forest. But before nightfall, the German troops returned to Bogdonova only to find them missing. Mina believes that the troops began looking for the women in all the nearby buildings since a soldier came to the barn before dark, entered it and began looking around. "As he climbed the ladder to the loft," Mina says, "I was sure I was going to die. I could see the soldier, who I recognized from Bogdonova, staring at the pile of hay." She is sure that he saw her and Shana Zelda. "After a moment of apparent pondering," Mina says, "the soldier went back down the ladder, left the barn and the area." Mina continues, "he was either blind or he discovered a conscience after the day's earlier brutality. Maybe, because he knew Shana Zelda and me from Bogdonova, he could not bring himself to send us to a certain death." Noah asks how she and his stepsister found the rest of the group and she replies that Solyzynsky came later that night and directed them to the hut. Drained by Noah's revelations, each in the group withdraws into his or herself to deal with their own grief and the guilt they feel for being alive. As much to give himself hope as to comfort Mina, Noah tells her, "don't give up, we will survive."

X

The next few weeks the group is busy hiding and surviving. Soon it is apparent that the area has become too dangerous because a number of farmers had seen them in and near the woods, and according to Solyzynsky, the Germans were offering rewards for leading them to Jews. The group decides it must move farther into the forest. After a brief discussion, the group decides to head towards the Berezina River near Bukatova. Mina tells them that the forest is much thicker there, it being the true beginnings of the Naliboki. Also she, at least, is a little familiar with the area because she had grown up on her father's farm which had been nearby. Most importantly, she says there are very few farmers living in the area because it is so isolated and among those that do, a few had worked for or did business with her father and might be willing to provide help. Finally, she says that unlike the people who lived near Bogdanova, the farmers near Bukatova would be less likely to recognize the others, if spotted, as being Jews from Vishnevo.

After a day of hiking and crossing the Berezina, they reach their destination. They then seek and find a thickly-wooded and overgrown area for a camp several kilometers away from the nearest paths and farms, but close to drinkable water. They construct rudimentary shelters with branches and leaves. They agree that this will be their home for the time being.

Quickly, they learn that their life here would not be easy. Being farther away from farms makes it more difficult to find food. The calendar is also moving into October, the beginning of the Russian winter, with its cold, freezing rain and occasional snow. They must not only beg and steal food but also old clothing to keep warm. Mina and Chiene are instrumental in keeping them alive. Chiene is a blond woman who can easily pass for a Gentile. She is able to obtain food and clothing from the locals without raising too much suspicion.

To help the group survive, Mina also approaches a local farmer named Samachvost who had done business with her father in the past. She asks him for help which he agrees to give explaining that her father had always been an honest and fair man. Samachvost says that Samuel Milikowsky showed kindness to his workers on the farm, even providing them medical care when they were injured, which was an unheard of act in the area. Samachvost provides Mina food and clothes for the group and even lets all the women visit the farm to bathe.

Other farmers are not helpful and must be threatened to obtain needed supplies. It is through such threats and force that the group obtains rifles left behind from World War I battles in the area or more recently by escaping Soviet soldiers and collected by the farmers. Notwithstanding the help and the weapons, the situation of the small band is becoming critical. They know they will not be able to survive the winter where they are. The ground is snow covered and the air is frigid. Starting fires is too dangerous and the cold is debilitating.

There are two opinions in the group on what they should do. Noah and the other men argue that they should go deeper into the Naliboki, live off the land, and try to join the Soviet partisans. The three women argue that they should go back to their hut in the forest near Bogdonova where food and shelter will be more readily available. Reasons why each approach is the more dangerous are put forth by all and agreement cannot be reached on a single approach.

Finally, the men say that they will head into the Naliboki. The women can choose to go with them or to the Bogdonova area. If the women choose the latter, the men say they will come back and get the women after joining the partisans. The women are terrified of the unknowns of the Naliboki and the partisans and choose the dangers of Bogdonova, which they at least comprehend. The men and women sadly part with little hope of seeing each other again.

The next two months for Noah and the other men are truly harsh. The weather is horribly cold and food is scarce. They live off roots and wild berries and the occasional rabbit or bird they can trap. By December 1942 they know they will either have to join the partisans or die. They go deeper into the Naliboki attempting to make contact.

Finally, when their hopes are at their lowest, they hear voices and the sound of men moving toward them. Noah's group lies low and remains quiet. Noah strains to hear the voices of those who are approaching. After a few moments, he makes out that they are speaking Russian. He then is able to see brief glimpses of figures wearing clothing that is largely Soviet army issue. Noah whispers to his friends that because he speaks the best Russian he will try to make contact with what he believes to be Soviet partisans but if they hear shots or shouts of trouble they should escape.

After moving quietly to within thirty meters of the partisans and remaining hidden, Noah calls out "Tovarish, don't shoot", at which point he slowly raises his arms in the air and then stands to face eight rifles pointing at him. The apparent leader of the partisan unit tells Noah, "raise your arms higher and move closer slowly." Noah complies. When Noah is within three meters of the leader, he motions two of the other partisans to search him for weapons. Finding none, the leader tells his men to keep a look out for others.

Next he starts to interrogate Noah. "I am called the major; who are you? Noah responds, "I am Naom Yacovlevich Podberesky," his name in Russian. "I was in a Soviet militia unit and was captured by the Germans near Minsk. I escaped and returned to my hometown Vishnevo but I decided to leave and join the partisans." The major asks Noah "where did you work before the German attack." Noah tells the Major about his job at the Soviet lumber operation and explains that he is a good communist. The major then says very pointedly, "you are not Russian; why did you really leave Vishnevo?" Noah realizes he has reached the point where his immediate fate will be sealed. He says, "Major, I am a Jew; all the Jews of Vishnevo were killed; only I escaped the slaughter. I can only survive with the partisans and it is the only place where I can seek revenge from the Germans. If you are also killing Jews, kill me now because the partisans are my last hope." The Major stares at Noah and says "we are not killing Jews and as long as you want to kill Germans, you can join our partisan unit. We are here looking for fighters." Noah feeling a sense of relief next tells the Major that he knows of two other small groups of Jews, which are made up of three men and three women, who want to join the partisans. The Major tells Noah to show him where they are and they will also be allowed to join if they are willing to fight. Noah tells the Major that the men are nearby and he will call them out. The Major tells Noah to tell his friends to come out with their arms in the air, which Noah does. After his three friends appear and are in turn searched by the partisans and questioned by the Major, the Major asks Noah where the women are. Noah replies that they are about 10 or 15 kilometers away near Bogdonova. The Major says that is farther than they had planned to go and the Bogdonova area is dangerous. Noah pleads that the women are in terrible danger and the men had promised to return for them if the partisans could be found. The Major agrees to get the women, and receives Noah's thanks. After being asked, the Major allows the men to retrieve their rifles which they had left in the brush.

XI

The Major questions the men about the exact location of the women. He also asks which man in Noah's group will be best able to take the partisans to the women at Bogdonova. Bare Michel is certain that he can and volunteers to go.

The Major next explains his plan. "Our group is too large to quietly get to Bogdonova and taking all of you could slow us down. I will go with the volunteer and four of my comrades. The rest of you will stay put and await our return. On the way, at Bukatova, we will pay two farmers, who have helped us before, to drive us in their horse drawn sleighs to Bogdonova. We will leave now and get there by nightfall and we will return tomorrow".

After the Major leaves, Noah and his friends begin a long tense wait. The remaining partisans share their food but are loathe to share any information about the partisans. The men make themselves as comfortable as they can on the cold night and get some sleep; however, the partisans are careful to have one man awake at all times acting as a sentry.

The morning brings no relief from the cold and as the time wears on, the group becomes a bit anxious. Late in the day, however, the group hears movement in the forest and soon several people appear. Noah becomes worried when he sees that the party arriving is made up only of one partisan, Bare Michel and Chiena. When the returning party joins their group, Noah asks Bare Michel and Chiena where Mina and Shana Zelda are. A separate conversation takes place between the partisans.

Bare Michel quickly tells Noah "everything is alright. The Major found his farmers and they took us on their sleighs to Bogdonova. I took the party to the hut where we found Shana Zelda and Chiena. We also found Lebke Rabinovich and Hershke Davidson there." Bare Michel explains that these two Jewish young men from Vishnevo had been hiding elsewhere in the woods for some time after escaping from Vigan. Chiena tells Noah that the two eventually joined the women with Solyzynsky's help.

Chiena then explains that about five weeks earlier Mina had left the group because of the cold and her hunger and begged Solyzynsky to let her hide in his house. Solyzynsky had agreed. Chiena continues "Shana Zelda begged the Major not to leave her best friend Mina behind. Mina had told Shana Zelda recently when bringing us food that she thought she would be found by the Germans soon since they visited the Solyzynsky farm often and more and more local people were becoming aware that Solyzynsky was hiding a Jew. The Major agreed to Shana Zelda's request and told her to let Mina know they would all leave the next day and she could join them. Shana Zelda went to tell Mina. The Major sent Bare Michel and me back since there would not be enough room in the sleighs for everyone the next day and he would want to move fast. Don't worry Noah, Shana Zelda and Mina will be here tomorrow with the Major."

Relieved, Noah reverts to waiting. The partisans have become a bit more open and provide some information about their unit and what they do. The partisans explain that they are members of the Chapievsky Brigade, one of a number of partisan units in the Naliboki all of which are commanded by General Platon. Their brigade is a fighting unit with few women. Deeper in the Naliboki are family units with more women and even children. There are even two Jewish family units, named after their leaders, Belsky and Zorin.

The partisans make it clear that for those who want to fight and kill Germans, their brigade is the best place to be. Their unit regularly mines railroad tracks and ambushes truck conveys. Their leader, General Kudrin, is a fair man and treats those who carry out their duties well. For those who do not, punishment is swift and severe. Most important to the partisans, they eat well and keep warm, and up to now the Nazis have not tried to enter the Naliboki to attack them.

Noah decides that the Chapievsky Brigade will be where he lives or dies. For Noah, the outcome matters little as long as he can kill Germans and collaborators along the way. His thoughts, however, return to Mina. He and the rest of the group resume their waiting. That night and the next morning pass uneventfully.

The group's concern gradually begins to mount as the next day wears on. By evening everyone, including the partisans, are worried. It is taking far too long for the Major to return, but there is nothing anyone can do except wait. One of the partisans says that if the Major does not return by day break, they will leave, since there will be no reason to wait any longer.

The group does not have to wait much longer. In the early hours of the next day a party is heard approaching the camp through the dark. Noah is quickly alert and sees immediately that the returning party is smaller than expected and several are wounded. As they get closer he sees that all the partisans have returned, although several have minor wounds. Instead of the four Jews Noah expects, only one other person is with them and it is Mina. She is suffering from a bad wound. She has been bleeding badly from the back of the thigh and her clothes are soaked in blood. She is not bleeding now, however, because bandages had been applied to stop the flow. The Major is helping her walk. Noah and others come to her aid.

The Major tells everyone that they were ambushed hours before on the way to Bukatova and while he does not believe they were followed, they must move quickly. He orders the entire group to move deeper into the Naliboki with partisans leading and guarding the rear of the column at his direction.

After hours of hiking through the thick forest and several stops to rest, the Major tells the Jews they are nearing the camp of the Chapievsky Brigade. The Major sends one of his partisans to another unit, the Staritzsky Brigade for help. The partisan is told to bring the doctor and nurse that unit has to the Chapievsky camp to tend to the wounded. From this last rest point it is not long until they reach the first sentries from the camp of the Chapievsky Brigade. Mina has kept up but is very weak from the loss of blood. As they enter the camp, General Kudrin and others witness their arrival. He orders that the wounded be moved to nearby huts and that they be treated. The other new arrivals are also directed to huts and told to eat and rest. Later, he would explain what was expected of them. Noah watches as Kudrin walks off with the Major who is briefing him.

Noah turns his attention to the hut where Mina has been taken and soon sees a doctor come with a nurse to tend to her. Later, as they leave Mina's hut, Noah approaches the doctor and asks how she is doing; the doctor says she should survive but he must now go and care for the wounded partisans but he would return and give him more information later.

When the doctor returns, he tells Noah that Mina has lost a good amount of blood from a shrapnel wound in her thigh. "Luckily," the doctor says "the shrapnel missed the bone and went completely through the thigh and I was able to clean the wound well, minimizing the likelihood of infection. With rest, she should recover."

The doctor asks Noah who he and the other new arrivals are and where they came from. Noah explains they are the only Jews from Vishnevo who were not killed by the SS. The doctor tells Noah that he and the nurse, who is his wife, are also Jews and like several hundred others in the Naliboki are the last of the hundreds of thousands of Jews who lived in the area around the Naliboki, including those who lived in larger cities like Minsk. Noah asks the doctor whether the Soviet partisans treat the Jews fairly. The doctor replies that the Jews in the Chapievsky and Staritzsky Brigades are not treated badly, but he cautions Noah that many of the Soviet partisans, including some officers, are anti-semites. He has heard that other units have killed Jews. He cautions Noah to always be on guard.

Changing the subject, Noah asks if he can go in and talk to Mina. The doctor says he will check her now before he leaves and if she is strong enough, Noah can see her. Several minutes after the doctor enters Mina's hut, he comes out and motions to Noah that he can go in, as the doctor takes his leave to return to his unit's camp.

Noah enters the hut and finds Mina awake and alert but ashen-faced and clearly devastated. Noah asks if Mina would like to talk. Mina says she does. Noah asks if it would be too difficult for her to discuss what happened. Mina replies, "Shana Zelda came to Solyzynsky's farm to get me in the morning and we returned to the woods. The Major was waiting with his sleighs. Shana Zelda, Lebke and I sat in the back of the first sled. Hershke sat next to the driver at the front. The Major stood on the runners of our sleigh and shouted directions to the driver. The other sleigh carried the rest of the partisans.

We had only traveled 5 or 10 kilometers and were on a cleared path through the trees. Suddenly, I heard a massive explosion and instantaneously felt a sharp pain. I was stunned for at least a few seconds when I felt myself being shaken. It was the Major. He was screaming at me that if I could move, he would try to help me escape. As my senses began to return, I heard rifle fire and grenades explode. Laying on top of me was Hershke covered in blood and dead. Next to me Lebke was also clearly dead. Shana Zelda was alive, but barely; her intestines were hanging out and, as the Major kept screaming at me to move out of the sleigh, she died too.

I got out of the sleigh after the Major pulled Hershke off of me grabbing my rifle as I went. The Major then ordered his men to follow him into the woods while returning the fire of the attackers. I remember running by our dead driver and his dead horse. For hours, we walked and ran through the forest with the Major using his compass to lead the way. After a while when we stopped to rest, the Major bandaged my thigh with an extra skirt I was wearing.

I do not know why I survived the attack and everyone else was killed. If Shana Zelda would not have thought of saving me she would not have died. I also do not know how I was able to keep up with the partisans in the forest. Nothing makes sense.

You, Noah, are a strong man who has had to work hard his whole life and serve in the army. It makes sense that you have survived. I was the daughter of a rich farmer and had people taking care of me my whole life. It just makes no sense."

Noah answers simply, "nothing that has happened makes sense and it is a waste of time trying to make sense of it. What does make sense is that we should fight to stay alive so that we can honor the memory of our family and friends and, if we are lucky, to take revenge upon those who took them from us. Noah takes his leave urging Mina to rest so that she can recover quickly.

XII

Noah finds life in the partisans to be tolerable. Food, clothing and firewood are plentiful. Everyone sleeps in huts or bunkers, under cover and protected from the snow, rain and cold.

Quickly, Noah and the other newcomers are briefed on what is expected of them. Each man is assigned to one of the three fighting companies of the Chapievsky Brigade. The women are assigned to the headquarters, with their major responsibilities being cooking, cleaning and taking care of supplies. Everyone, men and women alike, are assigned sentry duty about once per week and must cut and collect firewood. The men are also assigned to smaller fighting units for training on their military assignments. Noah is assigned to a small unit headed by a Russian soldier named Shartokin. The two other members of the unit, also Russian soldiers, are named Kolka and Mikael.

Shartokin explains to Noah that his unit is involved in three types of operations: obtaining food from the farmers in the area; blowing up trains; and, together with the rest of their company, ambushing German and police road traffic. Shartokin sets about to train Noah on placing the contact mines the unit uses to blow up trains. But Noah's first mission with the unit, and what would turn out to be a frequent one, is a food gathering assignment. His unit together with several others hike to a farm 10 to 15 kilometers away. They approach the farm in force with their rifles at the ready. The farmer and his family are asked for food for the partisans and, with no real choice, turn over a fair amount, including several pigs and chickens, potatoes, beets and grain. The partisans then carry the provisions back to their camp.

The food collected in these operations combined with some fruit and berries collected in the Naliboki ensure that the brigade eats well. Some of the potatoes and grain are also used to make vodka and samachon, a home made whiskey, thereby ensuring that the brigade drinks well between missions.

After a month, Shartokin tells Noah to get ready for his first mission to sabotage a railroad. The unit leaves at daybreak and hikes several hours to the edge of the Naliboki near an isolated spur of the Lida-Molidechno line. They position themselves in the woods several hundred yards beyond a bend in the tracks. Shartokin sends Kolka to position himself in the woods near the bend. He tells Kolka that a train is expected later that morning and that when he sees or hears it, he should warn them. Shartokin tells the group that Noah will be placing the mine on the tracks. Noah knows how the mine is to be activated but Shartokin repeats the instructions he gave Noah in training at the camp. Noah is also told that when he lays the mine he should make sure that it is positioned properly and is tied or weighted down so that it will not be dislodged by vibrations as the train approaches. When Shartokin finishes, Kolka moves up the tracks staying inside the tree line. Noah, Mikael and Shartokin remain hidden in the trees, keeping watch for any German patrols that might approach.

The group does not have to wait long. Kolka signals the approach of a train by whistling and Noah soon sees him running back toward them. Shartokin tells Noah "run out to the tracks and stay low just in case anyone is watching. Mikael and I will cover you from here. Once you have set the mine and activated it, get back here as fast as you can. If the train engineer sees you he may be able to stop the train. Some trains also have German soldiers acting as guards and you could be shot."

With that advice, Noah sets out as he is told. Being a fast runner, he reaches the tracks quickly. There Noah goes about his task methodically doing just as he has been told. As he is getting ready to activate the mine, he hears the first sound of the train, although the vibration of the tracks has been announcing its approach for some time. Noah finishes his job and runs as fast as he can back to the tree line, now no longer carrying the heavy mine or worrying about dropping the device. The group, now rejoined by Noah and Kolka, retreat a few more meters into the woods and wait.

Within seconds the train rounds the bend. It is being pulled by a steam engine which is trailed by five or six freight cars. Noah and his comrades wait and watch as the train approaches the mine at a moderate speed. Perhaps 50 meters short of the mine the engineer apparently sees the mine and applies the brakes. But it is too late and Noah sees the engineer jump from the engine just before the front wheel runs over the mine. At that instant, the front of the engine lifts off of the tracks and there is a terrific explosion. The engine and the cars following it run off the tracks falling on their sides.

Shartokin seeing enough to know that their mission is successful, and not wanting to face any German soldiers who might come from the train or be attracted by the noise, orders the group to leave quickly. After several kilometers of quickly moving through the forest, the group slows to a more leisurely pace, now secure that they are beyond the reach of any Germans who may have tried to follow them. Shartokin compliments Noah and the others on a job well done and the unit remains in good spirits as they return to the Chapievsky camp.

That evening Noah lays on his straw mattress, having trouble sleeping because of his exhilaration over the day's mission. He hears his comrades who share his hut whispering and his name is mentioned. Noah listens closely and hears one man whisper, "see I told you not to kill the Jew. He is steady and is willing to take on the dangerous jobs. I think he wants those jobs and that's better for us. If you would have killed him before for his boots, you would have been the one taking the risks out there today."

The next day Noah sees Mina and he tells her about the mission and the conversation that he heard at night. Mina is concerned about the conversation but Noah says he is not surprised by it and, in fact, it even gives him a sense of security. "As long as I take on all the dangerous jobs for my unit, the unit will do its best to protect me and keep me alive the rest of the time. I can sleep in peace and not worry about being shot in the back." Mina tells Noah to be careful and not to trust the Russian partisans too much, especially when they are drunk and their reason could be overcome by their hatred of Jews or their desire to take something he owned.

Over the next 18 months Noah goes on about 20 more successful missions blowing up trains. The early missions are much like his first but as the Germans grow weary of losing trains to the partisans, they begin building and manning watchtowers along the tracks. The partisans switch to more dangerous missions on moonless and cloudy nights. Eventually, the Germans virtually abandon rail transport in the areas along spur lines, concentrating their defenses on the mainline traffic supplying the Eastern Front, which by early 1944 has moved to within several hundred kilometers of the Naliboki. This leads to Noah's most difficult sabotage missions, which involve crossing several kilometers of open farmland at night to reach the mainline between Lida and Novogrudok, blowing up a guarded German supply train and returning to the protection of the Naliboki. With missions like this, by June of 1944, the Chapievsky Brigade and other partisan units in Belarus bring rail transport there to a virtual standstill, creating a dire supply situation for the German army.

XIII

As the winter of 1943 grows more bitter, a few additional Vishnevo Jews who had been hiding in the forests join the partisan unit. These include Bare Michel's daughter, Esther Rubin, Hershle Berman, Zhiske Podberesky, and Mina's cousin, Baruch Milikowsky. However, of these and the groups that originally arrived with Noah, only Mina, Zhiske, Hershle and Chiena Rabinovich remain with the Chapievsky Brigade. The rest either join or move on to other units, primarily the nearby Staritzky Brigade.

On a cold day, while Noah is serving sentry duty several hundred meters from the edge of the camp, he is visited by Mina, who has now fully recovered from her wound. She brings him a tin of hot soup and bread. They sit and talk. Mina tells Noah that she has been ordered to join the Staritzky Brigade and would be leaving later that day. Noah tells her he will be sorry to see her leave but that the two camps are close enough and interact enough that they will surely continue to see each other. Mina tells Noah she must confide in him before she leaves. Mina tells him "I had a dream several nights before in which my mother visited me and talked to me. She told me that you and I would survive the war and that we would be married." Noah answers her "your mother was a good woman and we must do everything we can to survive and make her right."

Later, after Mina leaves, Noah thinks of her and how much he will miss her. Those thoughts help him keep his mind off the cold, discomfort and boredom of his sentry duty. Fear keeps him awake, but not fear of a German attack. Rather, Noah knows the punishment if he is caught sleeping -- execution, which has already befallen another Jewish partisan who dozed off on guard duty.

When in camp, Noah's training with the partisans continues. He is assigned the job of being his company's machine gunner for ambushes. The training is not difficult, but carrying the Russian DP machine gun and its ammunition over great distances is taxing. The weapon itself weighs 10 kilos and must be carried on one's shoulder. The round, pie size, ammunition clips, which fit on the top of the weapon, weigh about 3 kilos each and Noah must carry three on his belt. All told, it means that on a mission covering a roundtrip of 20 kilometers or more through the thick forest, Noah must carry an extra 20 kilos. Making it worse, after each ambush, the partisans withdraw quickly to avoid the German troops that are likely to respond to the attack, making Noah's burden that much greater.

Notwithstanding the hardships of the assignment, Noah relishes it. Being made a machine gunner shows Noah the confidence his leaders have in his strength, endurance and fighting abilities. More importantly, it gives him a weapon that can spread more death among the Nazis and their collaborators.

Noah's first ambush mission takes place just as his leaders had planned and told him it would. Noah's company leaves camp hours before sunrise to allow for the set up of the ambush before first light. Kudrin selects an isolated spot on a road that the brigade has scouted and found often to carry German military traffic. The men are hidden in the woods on both sides of the road and fields of fire are established to ensure that the partisans do not shoot each other. Scouts are sent several kilometers up and down the road to keep watch and to warn the company about any strong German military force that might be a threat to the partisans.

At the ambush site, Noah's machine gun is placed in the best possible position, well-hidden and with a commanding view of the road. Noah is told by Kudrin to fire on the enemy only at his order. He is to shoot first at the drivers of any vehicles and then at any other occupants of the vehicles or any place they might be. The other partisans are told not to fire until they hear the distinctive sound of the machine gun. A few men are sent relatively close to the road with hand grenades and orders to use them to disable the vehicles.

The men then wait behind trees and in ditches for the traffic that day. Soon Noah hears the sound that other partisans have already heard and spread word about along the line -- the noise of truck engines. A few moments later, the first of what turns out to be three trucks comes into view around a bend about 200 meters away, traveling at a moderate speed slowed by the disrepair of the road. The trucks are covered and medium size with German army markings, similar to the trucks that brought the German troops to Vishnevo to slaughter its Jews. Though inwardly excited, Noah remains calm checking one last time that his machine gun is ready for its task.

Finally, as the three trucks reach the ambush spot, Kudrin gives Noah the order to fire and he does, immediately sending a spray of bullets into the lead truck's cabin hitting two German soldiers riding there. Next he moves his aim to the second truck continuing to fire and filling its cab, apparently occupied by just a driver, with bullets. Pausing only to replace his ammunition clip, Noah continues firing, moving his aim to the third truck but its cab is empty. Noah continues to move the gun sending shells into the side of the truck when he sees a German soldier, probably the driver, running back up the road towards the woods. Noah gets him in his sights and keeps him there as he fires. The German drops but Noah keeps firing at the body for several seconds after which he turns his attention back to the cargo areas of the trucks.

After what seems like hours, but in fact is only several minutes, the order to cease fire is given. For the first time Noah notices the full magnitude of the destruction wreaked by the partisans. The trucks have been totally destroyed. Partisans quickly move out to the road looking for weapons, supplies or anything else worth taking. The four German soldiers in the cabs are the only ones on the trucks and their bodies and the trucks are searched for military papers. Several partisans take watches and other valuables off the corpses. At this point, Noah is ordered to pack up and to prepare to return to the camp.

Kolka, who had passed Noah magazine clips during the ambush, asks Noah why he wasted bullets and time on the dead German lying in the road. Noah replies "I did not want him to get up and get away while I was not looking." Within minutes of when Noah is ready, Kudrin orders the company to pull back, many carrying supplies they have taken off the trucks. The officers push the partisans hard to move quickly away from the ambush site telling them that German army units could have been alerted by the noise and be nearby. They are not and, by nightfall, the company returns to camp.

Invariably, Kudrin's ambush missions are planned well and large German forces are avoided. Typically, the partisans encounter small German truck convoys or a solitary German field car. Sometimes all they encounter are local farmers or tradesmen who are deprived of some or all of their possessions but spared their lives. By May and June 1944, with the German army retreating, the number of ambushes increase and the number of German soldiers being encountered grows. It is on one of his last ambush missions that his company kills a particularly large number of German soldiers, including a Colonel. Noah takes the Colonel's automatic pistol as a reminder of a very good day.

XIV

Several months after Mina's transfer from the Chapievsky Brigade, Noah sees her return with a group bringing needed supplies from her camp. After unloading the supplies, the group leader tells Mina and the others that they will be returning to the Staritzky camp in several hours so they can rest. Mina and Noah go off alone to talk.

Mina tells Noah that she volunteered to come on the supply mission to see him. She asks how he is doing and he says he is fine. Mina tells Noah that she heard that he had contracted typhus and almost died. Noah assures her that he is fine, that he merely had to stay in bed several days and that he is now back to normal. Mina says, "I heard different from our nurse who treated you. She says you almost died from the fever, and that at one point you ran out of your hut delirious, without clothes, and threw yourself in the snow to cool off." Noah answers her with a shrug and explains that he does not remember much of what happened when he was sick. All I know is that right now I am fine and I've been cleared to go back on combat missions." Mina comments, "maybe you were better off sick." Noah replies, "so far our missions have been well planned and relatively safe; don't worry about me."

Noah, changing subjects, asks Mina how she is doing. She answers that she is also doing well. Her hours, she says, are taken up with cooking and cleaning and sentry duty. Discipline at her camp is severe but she says she is having no problems because she does what she is told. She tells Noah that one Jewish woman in her camp was recently executed for having sexual relations after being warned to stop. The woman apparently was spreading a venereal disease, which had incapacitated several men in the brigade. Mina says, "being a Jewish woman, its best to keep out of the way and away from trouble and do what you're told."

Noah next confides in Mina that he will soon be going on a very important mission. She asks where and he answers Vishnevo. "Why are you going there", she asks. Noah says the town is a good target, close to the forests and some distance from the nearest German troops. More importantly, the partisans believe the town has a number of Nazi collaborators who have taken action against the partisans and their friends. Among those targeted for death by the partisans are the mayor, Turunsky, the Chief of Police, and several police officers. Mina, knowing the part they played in the extermination of the Vishnevo ghetto agrees that they deserve to die.

Mina asks Noah what he will be doing on the mission. Noah answers that he will not be doing what he wanted, explaining, "Kudrin called me in to meet with the brigade's officers and told me about the mission. Knowing I was from Vishnevo he asked me to make a diagram of the town showing the police station and where the collaborators might be living, which I did. He also asked for good locations outside the town to set up ambushes in case the German soldiers at Bogdonova or Voloshin were to show up. I asked if I could play a part in the ambushes since it would be the best opportunity to kill Germans. But Kudrin told me I would be needed in the town since I knew its layout best and, more importantly, I could recognize the collaborators that were targets of the mission."

Mina tells Noah that this mission sounded dangerous. Noah agrees that it may be more dangerous than the others he has been on but it clearly is well worth the added risks. Mina begs Noah to be careful, to which Noah replies that he always is. Noah's happy time with Mina quickly comes to an end and Noah's mind turns back to anticipation for the Vishnevo mission, which has been all he has thought about since being told of it.

He only has several more days of waiting before the mission begins. Noah and several hundred other partisans are formed up in the morning for the mission. After marching several kilometers they are met by a number of horse drawn sleighs. With the sleighs, the partisans are able to make their way on paths through the forest to a spot several kilometers outside Vishnevo near the banks of the Alshanka river. They wait there resting until nightfall since the attack is planned for dark after the town is asleep.

A few hours after nightfall, Kudrin sends several units out with orders to set up ambushes on the roads leading to Vishnevo for any German attempts to reach town and to keep a lookout for any collaborators trying to escape after the partisan attack. Finally, they are told to cut the telephone lines just before midnight when the attack on the town would start.

The remaining partisans are broken into smaller units to attack the town's police station and government office, to search all the houses and buildings in the town for collaborators and needed supplies, and to burn the town to the ground before leaving. Noah's primary task is to find Turunsky and bring him back alive for questioning. Noah is assigned Kolka and Mikael to help him.

About 11 pm, the partisans remaining with Noah cross the river and quietly move toward the edge of the town. Noah tells Kolka and Mikael that Turunsky lives at the house of the town doctor and when the attack starts they will go directly there. Noah moves his group as close as possible to the doctor's house before the attack so that he and his men will only have to run about 50 meters to get to it when the attack starts.

At midnight the partisans start moving into the town from several directions. Noah and his men quickly get to the doctor's house and Noah breaks through the front door. The house is dark but Noah sees the doctor get up from a bed in the front room, startled by the noisy intrusion. Noah runs up to him pointing his rifle at his head and screaming "where is Turunsky." The doctor replies that he does not know. At this point, the sound of gunfire can be heard from the direction of the police station. Noah also can tell that his men are busy searching the room for valuables to steal, disinterested in the main mission. Noah calmly tells the doctor that he will either tell him where Turunsky is or Noah will put a bullet in his head. The doctor says nothing but points towards an adjoining room and then to the floor.

Noah knows that many of the houses in the town have storage cellars and he sets out looking for the trap door to the cellar in the adjoining room. Behind him he hears his comrades now threatening the doctor with a beating or death if he does not give them his watches, jewelry, gold and other valuables. Noah taps on the floor searching for the door in the dark. When he thinks that he has found it he bends down feeling for a handle. Upon discovering it, he steps back points his rifle toward the door and throws it open. As dark as the room is, the cellar and the ladder into it are even darker.

Before starting down the ladder, Noah hollers "Turunsky, I know you are there; come out with your hands empty." Getting no response Noah backs down the ladder with his rifle at the ready.

Upon reaching the bottom, Noah can see nothing because it is so dark. He also hears nothing except the gunfire in the town and the sounds of Kolka and Mikael threatening the doctor. Noah screams out "Turunsky, this is your last chance; come out now with your hands up or I will just start shooting now and make sure you are dead before I leave." At that moment, Noah hears a movement to his right and makes out the shape of Turunsky moving toward him slowly with his arms up. Turunsky says "Who are you and why do you want me"? Noah replies "I am with the Soviet partisans and my commander wants to talk to you." "But why me," says Turunsky, "I am only a school teacher." Noah answers "I know you, Turunsky; you are the mayor and you helped the Germans kill all the Jews in Vishnevo." "That is a lie; who told you this," Turunsky replies. Noah points the rifle at Turunsky's head and says, "nobody told me; I saw you with my own eyes helping the Germans kill the Jews. I'm the only Jew you didn't kill that day. You are lucky I don't kill you here and now. Move back as I climb the ladder and then you come up." After backing up the ladder and getting Turunsky out of the cellar, Noah gets the attention of his two comrades who he directs to tie up Turunsky's hands behind his back. They then take Turunsky out of the house and toward the police station where the partisan officers are expected to be. By now the firing in the town has stopped.

After delivering his prisoner, Noah sets out to determine if other collaborators have been killed or captured. He hears from other partisans that a policeman and the shoemaker have been killed but at least one other policemen had escaped. Noah makes a point of stopping at the druggist's house to confront him. Noah calls him out of his house with the intent of killing him. The druggist pleads for his life. Noah asks him why he was so happy on the day the Jews were killed and why he had to play music as they marched to their slaughter. The druggist answers that he had no idea that the Jews were being taken out of the ghetto to be killed. He also says that he had always had good relations with the Jews in the town and harbored no ill will toward them. He played music, he says, only to calm everyone. Noah decides to spare his life.

Next the partisans proceed to burn down the town. After setting the fires, they quickly pull out of town and retreat to the forest taking Turunsky with them for questioning. They are soon rejoined by all the other partisan detachments that were on the mission, and the force returns to camp.

Upon reaching their camp, Noah who has been guarding Turunsky, is told that the mission has been a success, he has done a good job, and the officers would begin Turunsky's questioning. Noah returns to his hut and later hears that the questioning did not go well. Turunsky did not cooperate and he repeatedly referred to his questioners as Stalinist bandits. For this affront, instead of getting a bullet to the back of the head, Turunsky is beaten to death with rifle butts.

XV

In late Spring 1944, Mina again visits Noah at the Chapievsky Brigade camp. They spend much of their time discussing the difficult time the partisans have had over the past six months. Mina and Noah tell each other of how they and their units had scattered and hidden deep in the Naliboki when they were attacked on two occasions by large forces of German and Ukranian troops. Noah tells Mina that at one point, while he was hiding in a swamp, neck deep in water, he could hear the Ukranian collaborator troops talking to each other and then hollering out in Russian urging the partisans who were hiding to surrender. "One group of Ukranians," Noah explains, "was hollering that the war was the fault of the Jews and that Russians should not die to protect Jews and communists. When I looked over to a partisan officer hiding with me, he was nodding in agreement."

Mina also has her story: "When the first German attack started, I was on sentry duty. I saw the Germans coming, fired off three or four shots and ran. It was the first time I ever fired a rifle. I don't think I hit anything. I'm surprised I could pull the trigger."

Noah says "the recent German operations against the partisans are a good sign. It means that we are hurting them so much that they must try to stop us. Lately we have been very busy attacking the railroads and road traffic."

Mina tells Noah, "there are strong rumors in my camp that the Soviet army will soon break through the German lines and retake our area. Radio reports have the lines only a few hundred kilometers east of the Naliboki and former Soviet soldiers in my unit tell me that once the breakout occurs, Soviet tanks could be here in days."

"We have the same rumors in our camp and I think they are true," Noah responds. "Our officers are getting their information and orders from Moscow and it looks to me like they are getting ready for a Soviet army advance."

Mina asks Noah what he will do after they are liberated. Noah responds that it is too early to make any plans. Furthermore, he is afraid that the Soviets will just put him in the regular army once they are liberated. If he can, he tells Mina, he will return to Vishnevo and he hopes she will as well. He tells her that once there, they can decide together what to do with their lives. They agree that it is too soon to make plans. Before long, Mina must leave Noah and return to her camp.

Several weeks later, one of his brigade officers enters Noah's hut at night and rouses the sleeping men. "The Soviet army has breached the German lines all along the front and are quickly moving west", he says. He orders the men to form up and prepare for combat.

For the next week Noah and the other partisans set up ambushes on roads near the Naliboki between Lida and Novgroduk. They attack any small groups of German soldiers they encounter. They are under orders to take prisoners for questioning, although Noah hears that some units are summarily executing captured prisoners and others are torturing them. Noah's unit captures one German officer and as ordered, returns with him to the camp. The officer refuses to answer any questions even with a partisan officer's gun to his head and he is shot.

Noah returns to his duties monitoring road traffic. Several days later, he hears approaching vehicles. Along with the loud noise of diesel engines, he hears the sound of falling trees. When the column comes into view, at first he fears it is a German Panzer tank unit moving toward them along the road and through the trees. Soon he sees the Soviet markings on the vehicles and his comrades recognize the vehicles as Soviet tanks. Noah's comrades are elated and one asks him why he is not celebrating along with them. He answers that he is happy to be alive but his happiness is tempered because he has lost much more in this war than most of his Russian comrades. It is late June 1944 and the partisan war in Belarus is over.

A week later, the Chapievsky Brigade is marched out of the Naliboki Forest and into Minsk. Noah can see that the city has been even more devastated by the war since he last saw it in 1941. In the city are tens of thousands of Soviet partisans who fought in Belarus for the past three years. Noah asks an officer what is going on and he is told that there will be a partisan victory parade soon in honor of Minsk's liberation and then the units will be disbanded.

Noah seeks out members of the Staritzky Brigade. Finding several camped nearby, he asks where Mina is. They tell him she became ill with pneumonia and was taken to a hospital somewhere in Minsk but they were not sure where. Noah is both relieved that Mina is still alive and worried about her illness.

The next day preparations are made for the victory parade. Medals for valor are awarded and Noah gets two to wear on his uniform. The parade is held before what is left of the war-weary, depleted population of Minsk. After the parade and back in camp, the partisans are lined up before tables where officers are sitting. Each man approaches a table for his brigade and gives his name. The officer checks a ledger and tells him what he is to do. Baruch

Milikowsky in a line near Noah's approaches the table for the Staritzky brigade and is given his orders. He walks past Noah and tells him that he has been ordered to report to a Soviet army mechanized infantry unit outside the town.

Noah soon reaches the front of his line. When he approaches the table, the officer looks up and says "Naom Yacovlevich here are your orders. Your war is over." Noah looks at the discharge papers and slowly walks away surprised that he is not being sent to the front.

After turning in his weapons, as is required of all the discharged partisans, and saying goodbye to his comrades, Noah begins his journey back to Vishnevo, because that is what he told Mina that he would do and because he really has no other choice. Walking and hitching rides on Soviet army vehicles, he reaches Vishnevo the next day, finding that a number of the buildings burned by the partisans had been rebuilt or repaired and several had survived the fires.

Upon entering the town he approaches a local woman on the main street and asks if any Jews have returned and if so where are they living. She looks at him with fear, as if he had just returned from the dead seeking revenge, and points to a house down the street which Noah recognizes as being formerly the home of a Jewish family murdered by the Nazis. Noah approaches the house and knocks on the door. It is opened but only a crack until the occupant sees it is Noah and then lets him in. Inside Noah finds six other Vishnevo Jews who had survived in the forests, but Mina is not among them; no one has seen her since she was taken to the hospital in Minsk. Noah is distraught but the others console him and convince him that Mina will return as soon as she is able to leave the hospital. Noah can only hope and wait for her.

XVI

Noah's wait lasts only for a few days. Mina returns to Vishnevo then and finds the house where the Jews are living. Her return lifts a heavy weight from Noah and he feels real happiness for the first time in many years. Everyone wants to know what happened to Mina after she arrived in Minsk.

Mina proceeds to tell her story. "I was taken to a hospital and was treated there for a high fever and a bronchial infection. After several days I started getting better but the doctors would not let me leave. Then one night, a few days ago, the German air force bombed Minsk and a few bombs came close to the hospital. I decided it was too dangerous and I had to leave. I dressed and took my rifle and supplies and left the hospital. After walking about a kilometer, I was stopped at a Soviet army checkpoint and the soldiers began questioning me.

They told me that all the partisans had been disarmed and had left the city and no civilian was supposed to have a rifle. The soldiers took my rifle and took me back to the hospital to confirm my story. A nurse there vouched for me. After the soldiers left, I offered the nurse my canteen, which was full of pig fat I brought from the forest, if she would take me to the road to Vishnevo since I could not find the way on my own. She accepted my offer and when we got to the road, I joined several other women who were going to Voloshin and hitched a ride on top of a Soviet army fuel truck which dropped me off here. I had promised the drivers that they could spend the night in my father's house when we got here. Of course, the house is no longer standing and they drove on. I am just glad I am with friends."

When the group finishes its questioning, Noah and Mina go off for a more private conversation. Noah asks Mina how her last days with the Staritzky Brigade had gone before the liberation. Mina replies "it was a very difficult time for me. The unit captured three German enlisted soldiers, all three just teenagers. I was assigned to guard them. They were with us for about a week and I had several conversations with one of them. One day we had him chopping firewood while I guarded him. As I watched him I remembered one of the last things my younger brother, Moshe, told me after he had spent the day at slave labor chopping wood for the Germans at Bogdonova. Moshe said that his only wish was that one day he would be watching the

Germans chopping wood for us. He never got his wish, dying several days later when all our families were killed.

As I watched the German soldier, I thought of Moshe and cried, but I could only feel sorry for the German soldier. Later that day, he showed me a picture of his family and then he told me he knew he was going to die and that I should take his ring, better that I should have it than those who killed him. I told him I could not take his ring and I didn't know anything about him dying, but I really did know. Later I begged my commander to relieve me of guard duty, and the next day I heard they marched the three boys out into the forest, had them dig their own graves, and shot them in the back of the head. With all the death and misery caused by the Nazis, I should not feel bad, but I do."

Noah replies that now that the war is over for the two of them, they will have to learn to live with many bad memories. "The important thing now," Noah says, "is to start a new life and find new reasons to live. For me, you are the best reason to live and I hope you feel the same way about me. I want you to marry me and for us to start a family and have a future." Mina does not hesitate in agreeing.

They tell the rest of the group and set a wedding date a few weeks off so that they can obtain the things they will need to get married -- a prayer book, a ring, and wine for the required blessings. Since there were no rabbis left alive near them, they decide that one of their group would perform the ceremony.

The following two weeks in Vishnevo are very difficult for Noah and Mina. They see former Jewish homes being occupied by non-Jews who had been their neighbors. They also see people on the street wearing clothes that once belonged to them or their families. A few non-Jews approach them to return items they had taken or to give them food and clothing as a form of compensation or a sign of compassion. On their own, Noah and Mina approach the people who had taken their fathers' two dairy cows and take them back.

Several non-Jews warn Noah and Mina that the AKA is still operating in the area and is still intent on killing Jews. In particular, Noah is a target because of his activities with the partisans. The warnings are well founded. On a regular basis at night, shots are fired at the house where the Jews are staying. One of the group, Yashke Rabinovitz, Chiena's husband, is murdered nearby in cold blood while trying to acquire food. Chiena, who now has a young baby, is left mourning one more death. At this point, the group decides it is too dangerous to stay in Vishnevo and they must move to Bogdonova, where a Soviet army detachment is stationed. Staying there will provide some protection from the AKA.

So after returning and being back for less than a month, the last Jews to live in Vishnevo pack up and leave at the end of July 1944. While not being greeted with open arms at Bogdonova, at least there they feel a small degree of safety. On August 1, Noah and Mina are married at Bogdonova, with a borrowed ring and a tattered prayer book, and the group toasts the couple with a few drinks of the little bit of Vodka they have acquired. They celebrate the wedding, which they make a happy occasion despite the misery and suffering they have all endured.

XVII

Because of his work experience for the Soviets in 1940 and 1941 and his status as a decorated veteran, Noah is given the job of running a mill near Bogdonova. By Soviet standards, the job is a good one. Farmers are required to bring their entire grain harvests to the mill and in return Noah gives them script to purchase items and flour based on the weight of the grain brought in. Because Noah reads the scales, the farmers treat him well, often giving him a chicken or vodka to encourage him to read the scales particularly well.

Noah's and Mina's lives remain empty and risky and they are constantly haunted by the memories of their dead families. Regularly Noah and Mina are warned that the local AKA unit has ordered Noah's death. The Jewish community they knew from before the war is gone. Nothing is left to keep them in the area and they soon decide that they will do all they can to leave Belarus and, hopefully, get to Israel where they both have family.

Months go by, however, before Noah's and Mina's plans to leave are anything but dreams. The war goes on in Poland and Germany, making civilian travel impossible and the authoritarian Soviet government requires special papers of anyone wishing to travel. Such papers must be obtained from the local military authorities and are virtually impossible to acquire. All Noah and Mina can do is bide their time. They do send letters to their close relatives in Palestine -- Noah to his sister, Chana Alon, and Mina to her mother's parents, the Dickensteins, and to her father's brother, Zev Milikowsky -- letting the family know they had survived, while the rest of the family had been killed. Receiving no response, they can only wonder if the mail got through.

Finally, Noah and Mina's prayers are answered. The Soviet government issues an order permitting persons who consider themselves to be Polish, and who reside in the portion of Belarus that had been a part of Poland before the war, to move west across the new Polish border. Noah and Mina see this as a chance to leave a land with memories of death and start a new life. They are convinced that once in Poland and out of the Soviet Union, they will be able to emigrate to Israel. The next day Noah and Mina apply for their travel papers.

While waiting for their travel papers, Noah and Mina's character and courage are tested one last time. A relative of Solyzynsky comes to their house. She tells them that Solyzynsky has been arrested by the NKVD, the Soviet secret police, and accused of being a German collaborator. Noah asks why the NKVD would do this and the woman tells Noah that Solyzynsky has enemies that lied to the authorities about him. Noah then asks the woman what she wants of them and, in response, she begs them to go to the NKVD and testify that Solyzynsky is a good Soviet citizen and that any stories to the contrary are lies. Noah, remembering the kindness shown to Jewish survivors, and especially Mina, by Solyzynsky and the risks he took for them, agrees to the woman's request.

The next day Noah and Mina go to the Soviet army headquarters at Bogdonova and ask to speak to the commander about Solyzynsky. They are taken into an office where the commander and the NKVD head for the area await them. Asked their reason for being there, Noah explains that they are there to vouch for Solyzynsky and to assure the authorities that he was never a collaborator. In response, the NKVD head angrily asks Noah and Mina who they are to vouch for anyone and why should the authorities believe them. Noah tells the Russians that he and his wife had been Soviet partisans and he had been decorated. He continues by explaining how Solyzynsky had risked his life by hiding Mina and providing help to several other Jews who the Nazis were hunting.

The NKVD chief scoffs at Noah's arguments. "Solyzynsky was well off before the Nazis arrived and he did well while they controlled the area. Maybe he helped a few Jews for their money, but he turned many Jews and communists over to the Nazis as well," the NKVD chief says. Noah responds that he knows of no person betrayed by Solyzynsky to the Nazis but many that he helped save. And in reply, the NKVD chief says, "why should I believe you; maybe you were also a collaborator and should be in custody." Noah looks at the two men directly and says "I was a Soviet partisan and I am sure I killed more Nazis in this war than both of you. I was not a collaborator and neither was Solyzynsky. In fact, in this area, he was one of only a few who did anything against the Nazis."

Noah stands unsure of whether he has gone too far. The Soviet commander and NKVD chief whisper to each other as Noah waits. The commander rises from his seat and addresses Noah. "You have taken a huge risk coming here. Your words are owed some respect. Solyzynsky will be released." Noah and Mina leave, relieved that they had accomplished their task and that they were not imprisoned.

Several weeks later, Noah and Mina get their travel papers to leave the Soviet Union and enter Poland. They go about selling all their property which amounts to a little furniture and their two cows. With some of the money they receive, they buy railroad tickets to Bialystok just across the border in

Poland. The rest of the money is in gold rubles which Noah sews into his clothes. Noah puts his medals in their pillow which had belonged to Mina's parents and which she had retrieved from the person living in her parents' farmhouse at Bukatova. When Noah and Mina board their train at Bogdonova, over 300 years of a Jewish presence in the area comes to an end.

XVIII

Noah and Mina only spend a short time in Bialystok. Jews there tell them that Jewish authorities are in Poland helping refugees leave the area of Soviet occupation but that they are located farther west in Poland in the larger cities. As suggested, Noah and Mina take the next train to Lodz, southwest of Warsaw.

In Lodz, they are directed to an office run by Jews from Palestine who are in Poland helping refuges. Noah and Mina explain they have family in Palestine and want to emigrate there. They are told that no new Jews are being allowed to enter Palestine legally and the British are intercepting boats carrying illegal Jewish emigrants and returning them to Europe or taking them to Cyprus. Noah and Mina are encouraged to move on to a displaced persons camp in Germany or Austria to make their travel to Palestine easier once such travel is possible. They agree and are given false papers showing that they are Greek refugees. They are told to feign an inability to speak or understand Polish and Russian and are further told to get rid of any possessions they are carrying that would give away their true identities or origins. Finally, they are given train tickets to Lindz, Austria, by way of Bratislava, Czechoslovakia, and some money for food.

On their way to the train station in Lodz, Noah throws his Soviet medals off a bridge into the river below. He is still proud of the medals, but if he were to be caught with them by the Soviets while carrying Greek papers, he and Mina would likely be imprisoned.

The Greek papers serve Noah and Mina well crossing the Polish, Czech and Austrian borders, all controlled by Russian troops. Apparently, the sight of Greek slave laborers heading south towards home from Poland and Germany is not uncommon. Upon arrival in Lindz in the late summer of 1945, Noah and Mina are directed to the Trofea displaced persons camp where they are assigned quarters and make connections with the Jewish underground officials in the camp, again expressing their desire to emigrate to Palestine.

While at Trofea, Noah and Mina again send letters to their close family in Palestine letting them know they are alive. Noah also writes to his mother's brother who emigrated to up-state New York at the turn of the century. Most excitingly, Mina discovers at Trofea that she is pregnant and will be having a baby in March 1946.

After spending six weeks at Trofea, the Jewish underground tells Noah and Mina that if they are willing, they can be smuggled into Italy from which transport to Palestine will be easier. Young couples, especially those where the wives are pregnant, are being given some priority. Noah and Mina agree. Several days later they are given train tickets to Padua, Italy. They are told that the Austria-Italy border is more closely guarded because it marks the end of Soviet control, but the border guards had been bribed and passage would be easy. It does not turn out this way, however. The bribed border guards are not on duty when Noah and Mina's train reaches the border. The Jewish refugees on the train are warned and told to jump off the stopped train and run for the border, which Noah and Mina do with several others. After running several kilometers, they encounter several farmers who tell them they are not heading for Italy; rather, they are moving toward Yugoslavia, which is ruled by its own communists. The refugees turn but they are soon captured by the border police who return them to the railroad line where they are put on the first train back to the Trofea camp.

The experience is heartbreaking to Noah and Mina, but two weeks later, they are offered the chance to go to Italy again. This time they are successful, reaching Padua and from there, sent on to the displaced persons camp in Cremona, southeast of Milan.

Cremona is a small town in a farming region famous for Stradivarius and his violin making. The displaced persons camp is housed in an old government building with a courtyard about a kilometer from the town center which dates back to the middle ages. Noah and Mina register as Polish refugees at the camp, which is run by the United Nations. They also register their names with the Red Cross, which circulates lists of holocaust survivors around the world. Noah is placed in a training program for truck mechanics but spends most of his time playing volleyball with other men in the camp. Mina prepares to have a baby.

Within weeks of arriving at the Cremona camp, Noah and Mina begin to receive letters from their families. The best news comes from Palestine. Mina's grandparents have received word that Baruch, Mina's brother is alive with the rest of the Mir Yeshivah in Shanghai, China. The letter says he traveled across Russia and then to Japan before being interred by the Japanese in 1942 in Shanghai for the duration of the war. Baruch is waiting in Shanghai for passage to the United States.

Unfortunately, the letters from Palestine also indicate that the situation there is not good both politically and economically. A guerrilla war is going on among the Jews and Arabs and by the Jews against the British who govern the land. Jewish émigrés are still being turned away from Palestine and the family says life is very difficult for those who are there. Noah and Mina see no other alternative, so their hope remains to emigrate to Palestine. They bide their time.

In March, Mina gives birth to a baby boy who they name Samuel after Mina's father. The baby is healthy and Mina recovers quickly, walking the kilometer from the hospital to the displaced persons camp two days after Samuel's birth. Noah and Mina and their friends in the camp gather eight days later for the baby's circumcision and to celebrate the new baby and in a way the survival of the Jewish people.

Noah continues with his mechanics training and Mina busies herself with caring for her new son. Meanwhile, they begin to correspond with Baruch who is now in the United States. Baruch says there is a possibility that he can get U.S. Immigration papers for Noah and Mina if they are interested. They respond that they want to go to Palestine but if they cannot, the United States is their next choice. They tell Baruch to do what he can.

Later in 1946, Noah receives a letter from his sister in Palestine telling him that Shimon Peres, who was born in Vishnevo and emigrated to Palestine in the 1930's, would be in Milan in several weeks on business. The letter says that the family in Palestine would be sending letters and some money with him for Noah and Mina and it provides a time and place for Noah to meet Shimon in Milan.

Noah makes arrangements to travel to Milan to meet Shimon. Noah and Mina know that Shimon has an influential position with the Jewish leadership in Palestine and they decide this will be a good opportunity to establish whether emigration to Palestine is a realistic goal.

Upon reaching Milan, Noah meets Shimon at his hotel and they go to a café to talk. Shimon gives Noah the letters he is carrying and asks Noah about the last days of the Jewish community in Vishnevo and Voloshin where Shimon had lived. Noah tells him of the many relatives and friends of Shimon that the Nazis had killed and how they had perished. Noah asks Shimon about the situation in Palestine and whether there is any chance that Mina and Noah would be allowed to go there soon. Shimon tells Noah that emigration to Palestine will be virtually impossible until a Jewish state is established there. Shimon also tells Noah that he believes that the British will leave Palestine and that the Jews there will eventually be given their own state, but that could take a year or more. According to Shimon, statehood could also lead the Arabs to start a war. Noah parts company with Shimon knowing that Mina and his dream to emigrate soon to Palestine is unrealistic.

During the next six months, Noah and Mina work with the refugee agencies in Cremona and correspond with Baruch to arrange for a visa to enter the United States. The most important step, getting an employer to provide a job for and sponsor Noah, is accomplished by Baruch who has by now become a Rabbi. The Jewish school where Baruch is teaching offers Noah a job as a Hebrew and religious studies teacher. With the sponsorship in place, emigration to the United States becomes a matter of paperwork and time.

In early 1947, Noah and Mina get word that their immigration paperwork has been approved and they should travel to the U.S. Consulate in Rome to get their final documentation. The refugee authorities provide them with train tickets to Rome and Naples, from which they will embark to the U.S., and some money on which to live. Later, after Noah, Mina and Samuel get their travel papers, the refugee authorities arrange for passage to New York on the *Marine Perch*, an old liberty ship still painted in its wartime colors.

In July 1947, two weeks after setting sail from Naples and after stopping in several ports on its voyage, the *Marine Perch* enters New York harbor. Noah and Mina marvel at the Statute of Liberty and the skyscrapers of Manhattan. As the *Marine Perch* turns to head up the East River to a pier, Noah and Mina contemplate the end of their nightmare and the beginning of a new life as they look out on the many American flags flying from the buildings and piers lining the New York shoreline.

XIX

American flags are resplendent on a sunny hot day 50 years later at the Navy-Marine Corps Stadium of the U.S. Naval Academy in Annapolis, Maryland. The stadium is full that day with the family and friends of the members of the Naval Academy graduating class, soon to be sworn in as U.S. Navy and Marine officers. On stage at one end of the field are the many dignitaries in attendance including Vice President Gore who will be giving out diplomas and commissioning documents to the graduates. Sitting directly in front of the stage are the 1,000 graduates in their starched dress white uniforms. To their side on the field is a section for VIPs, some of whom are also relatives of graduates. In the stands that line the sides of the field are the rest of the attendees including the remaining 3,000 midshipmen who had begun the formalities by marching into the stadium.

For the most part, the inhabitants of the VIP section look like a cross section of America. Clearly, however, people in uniform make up a substantial percentage of the people there. Minorities are underrepresented. One row looks and sounds different in its own way. Sitting in this row is Noah Podberesky, now 82 years old. Next to him on one side is his wife, Mina, and on the other side their son Sam, who is now 50. Next to Sam is his wife, Rosita, and next to her is her 75 year old mother Hela Rubinstein. Sitting next to Mina is Lt. Daniel Podberesky, Sam's and Rosita's oldest son, dressed in his U.S. Air Force uniform. In addition to the decidedly European look of the three oldest members of this group, the fact that they are the only people speaking Yiddish in the stadium sets them apart.

Sam spends some of his time explaining the ceremony to his parents and mother-in-law, having to use his Yiddish and Spanish to converse with his mother-in-law, who like his parents, had survived the holocaust but emigrated to Costa Rica after the war. After the invocation and the playing of the National Anthem and the Navy and Marine Corps Anthems, Sam turns to his father and tells him to look up over the stage, that something exciting and impressive was about to happen. At that moment, the ceremony pauses; the noise level decreases in the stadium for a moment; then a low roar can be heard in the distance far behind the stage; the roar begins to build quickly and the crowd stands to get a better view; and within seconds the roar becomes deafening and all look up to see four Navy F-14 Tomcat fighter/bombers, in a tight diamond formation, fly 500 feet over the stage and the stadium at 400 miles per hour. The crowd stands and cheers lustily and then take their seats for the rest of the ceremony.

Noah stands with everyone else as the jet crescendo begins to mount, but his mind begins to wander to an earlier memory. He is mounted on a horse on the edge of a forest in Poland. Next to him is a Polish cavalry colonel, who is telling him to be quick to blow the officer's bugle command to charge when ordered. Surrounding them are hundreds of other mounted Polish cavalry troops. In front of them is an open field and perhaps 500 meters away spread across the field are hundreds of German foot soldiers and several armored cars heading towards the forest. The roar of German Junkers and Stuka bombers can also be heard and their noise is getting louder.

Suddenly, three Jenkal bombers fly over the German troops and the Polish cavalry hiding under the trees, apparently without taking any notice of them. The Polish cavalry maintain their discipline while controlling their horses. However, the next sound they hear a few moments later is the high pitched whining of Stuka dive bombers attacking their position. Noah finds bombs exploding all around him. One kills his colonel and his horse and knocks Noah to the ground dazed. He regains full consciousness only to recognize that his unit has been devastated. He stands and finds himself in the midst of dead and dying horses and men and staring into the barrel of a lugar held by a Wermacht officer who is screaming at him in German.

At this point Noah feels a tap on his shoulder and he is back on a sunny field in Annapolis. Sam is telling him "Dad, I think Michael is next; try to get a better look." Noah stares at the stage. The roll call of graduates continues in alphabetical order with each graduate walking up onto the stage, receiving his diploma and shaking the hand of the Vice President. The speaker then calls out "Michael Podberesky" and a 21 year old figure climbs the steps to the stage; from a distance he looks like his grandfather, Noah, same height and build. He crosses the stage like so many before him and after shaking the Vice President's hand he holds up the diploma in a sign of success and joy.

Sam turns to look towards his father and says "Dad, you never thought you'd have two grandsons that are officers, did you?" Noah answers, "they are good boys and they know we owe this country a lot." Sam then notices a tear under his father's eye. "You must be really happy, Dad; I can't say I ever remember you crying," Sam says. Noah hesitates a second and answers, "I'm lucky son, if I was a crier, I would have run out of tears long ago."

NOAH PODBERESKY AS A TEENAGER WITH HIS FAMILY
This picture of the Podberesky/Abramovitch family was taken in Vishnevo in the early 1930s. It is the earliest picture of Noah Podberesky who is seated at the left. Next to him from left to right are Noah's father, Yacov (Jacob) Podberesky; Noah's stepsister, Shana Zelda Abramovitch; Noah's stepmother, Minke (Abramovitch) Podberesky; Noah's stepbrother, Zimke Abramovitch; Noah's stepsister, Golde Abramovitch; a friend of Golde, whose last name was Davidson; and Noah's brother, Noteh Podberesky.

A TEENAGE MINA PODBERESKY
This picture was taken in Vishnevo c 1934. It is the earliest picture of Mina Podberesky, who is standing at the right dressed in the uniform of the Shomaer Hatzair Zionist Youth Group. Next to her from right to left are her cousins, Isser and Menachim Gitlitz, and her siblings, Resele and Moshe Milikowsky.

THE PODBERESKY FAMILY PRE WORLD WAR II

This Podberesky family picture was taken in Vishnevo c 1934 on the occasion of the upcoming emigration of Tuvia Eliovich (later changed to Alon) and his wife, Chana (Podberesky) Eliovich, to Israel. Noah Podberesky is not in this picture because he was away at a zionist youth camp when the picture was taken.

Back Row, Left to Right - Zev Dudman and his wife, Sarah (Podberesky) Dudman; Gedalia Podberesky; Noteh Podberesky, holding his son, Chaim; Chana (Podberesky) Eliovich and her husband, Tuvia; Rezele Stoller, her husband, Kalman, and their son, Echiel.

Middle Row, Left to Right – Moeshke Dudman, Zev's and Sarah's son, Chaike (Rabinovich) Podberesky, Noteh's wife; Batye (Podberesky) Podberesky, Gedalia's wife; Itcha Ber (Zvi Dov) Berkman; Yacov Podberesky and his wife, Minke (Abramovitch) Podberesky; and Zimke Abramovitch, Minke's son from her first marriage.

Bottom Row, Left to Right – Grunia, a friend of Sarah Dudman, last name unknown; Grunia's brother; Nechama Dudman, Zev's and Sarah's daughter; Nechemia Eliovich (later changed to Alon), Tuvia and Chana's son; Chaimke Podberesky, Noteh's son; Avramela Podberesky, Noteh's son; Shana Zelda Abramovitch, Minke's daughter from her first marriage.

Relationships to Noah and Mina Podberesky

Itcha Ber Berkman was Noah's grandfather. Itcha Ber's daughter, Nechama (Naomi), was Yacov Podberesky's first wife and was Noah's mother. She died in the late 1920s. Sarah Dudman, Chana Eliovich, Gedalia Podberesky and Noteh Podberesky were Noah's siblings. Chaike (Rabinovitch) Podberesky, in addition to being Noah's sister-in-law, was also the sister of Chana and Yehoshua Rabinovitch, who are pictured elsewhere with the Milikowsky family, and a cousin of Mina. The Stollers were cousins of Noah. Minke Abramovitch was Noah's stepmother and Zimke Abramovitch was his stepbrother. Shana Zelda Abramovitch, in addition to being Noah's stepsister, was Mina's best friend.

THE MILIKOWSKY FAMILY

This picture was taken at the Milikowsky family farm at Bukatova near Vishnevo c 1936. It was taken when Avrum Dickenstein, Mina (Milikowsky) Podberesky's uncle, came from Israel to take his sister, Matla (Dickenstein) Gitlitz and her two children back with him. Matla's husband had recently passed away and her parents and all her siblings except for Mina's mother Malka (Dickenstein) Milikowsky had immigrated to Israel several years earlier.

Standing in the back row from left to right are Baruch and Eliochim Milikowsky, Mina's brothers; Mina; Chiena Rabinovich; Matla (last name unknown), Mina's cousin; Sheva Shinshilevich, a friend of Matla (the cousin); Yehoshua Rabinovich, Mina's cousin who later became Mayor of Tel Aviv and Finance Minister of Israel; and Avrahom Milikowsky, Mina's brother.

Sitting on chairs from left to right are Samuel Milikowsky, Mina's father; Nathan Milikowsky, Mina's brother, who is sitting on the lap of Mina's mother Malka (Dickenstein) Milikowsky; Avrum Dickenstein; and Matla (Dickenstein) Gitlitz.

Sitting on the ground from left to right are Resele Milikowsky, Mina's sister; Moshe Milikowsky, Mina's brother; and Isser and Menachim Gitlitz, Matla Gitlitz's sons.

NOAH PODBERESKY IN THE POLISH ARMY
This picture, which was taken in 1937 or 1938, shows Noah Podberesky in his Polish Army uniform. Because of his musical talents Noah spent most of his time in the army as a coronet player in an army band. As Poland mobilized for a possible war with Germany in 1939, he was reassigned as a bugler to a Polish cavalry unit.

THE NEW PODBERESKY FAMILY POST WORLD WAR II
This picture was taken in Cremona, Italy in 1946. It is the first picture of the author, taken when he was about 8 months old, flanked by his father, Noah, who was then 31, and his mother, Mina, who was 25.

NOAH PODBERESKY AS A CANTOR

This picture of Noah Podberesky was taken in the early 1950s and was used in a Baltimore synagogue advertisement for Jewish High Holiday services. When Noah first arrived in Baltimore, he began to work as a cantor in local synagogues using the name Noah Persky. Noah learned cantorial music and how to lead religious services from his father, who led services in one of the Vishnevo synagogues, and later when he sang in the choir of the Vilna City Synagogue under the direction of Cantor Simcha Kusevitzky. Noah gave up the cantorial profession when he realized he could not make a living from it.

www.ingramcontent.com/pod-product-compliance
Lightning Source LLC
Chambersburg PA
CBHW031648040426
42453CB00006B/247